ÆON FLUX

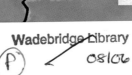

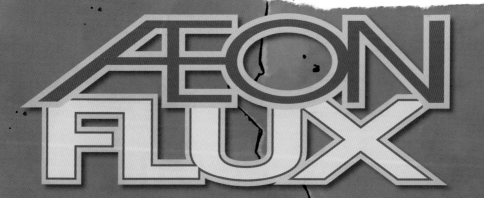

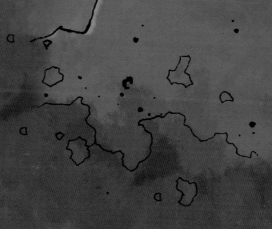

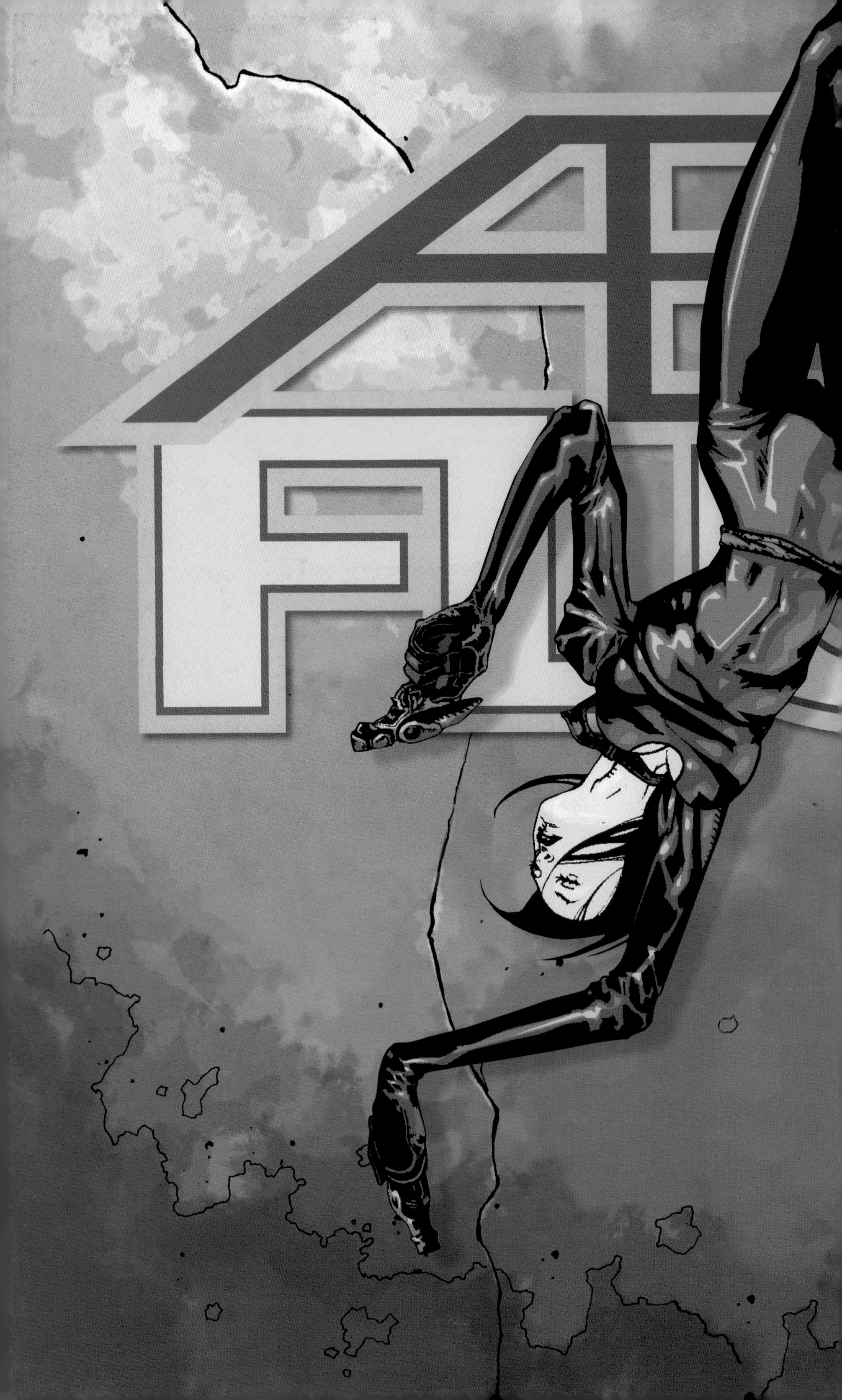

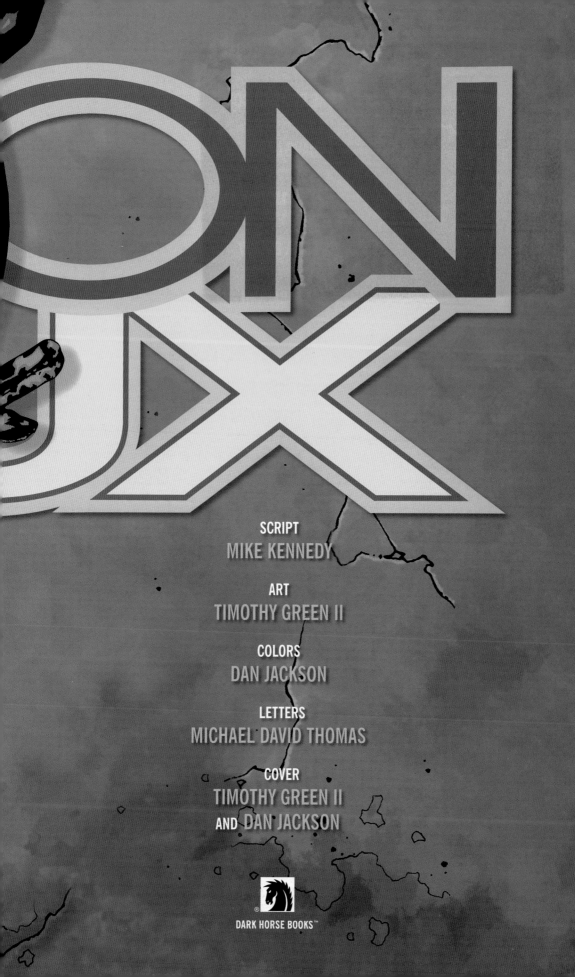

ONYX

SCRIPT
MIKE KENNEDY

ART
TIMOTHY GREEN II

COLORS
DAN JACKSON

LETTERS
MICHAEL DAVID THOMAS

COVER
TIMOTHY GREEN II
AND **DAN JACKSON**

DARK HORSE BOOKS™

PUBLISHER
MIKE RICHARDSON

EDITOR
DAVE LAND

ASSISTANT EDITOR
KATIE MOODY

DESIGNER
DEBRA BAILEY

ART DIRECTOR
LIA RIBACCHI

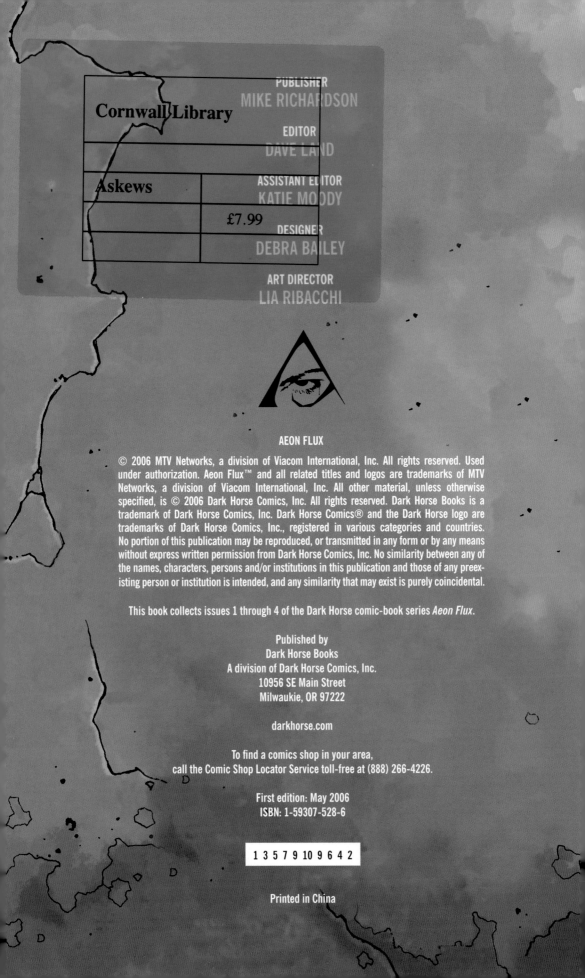

AEON FLUX

This book collects issues 1 through 4 of the Dark Horse comic-book series *Aeon Flux*.

Published by
Dark Horse Books
A division of Dark Horse Comics, Inc.
10956 SE Main Street
Milwaukie, OR 97222

darkhorse.com

To find a comics shop in your area,
call the Comic Shop Locator Service toll-free at (888) 266-4226.

First edition: May 2006
ISBN: 1-59307-528-6

1 3 5 7 9 10 9 6 4 2

Printed in China

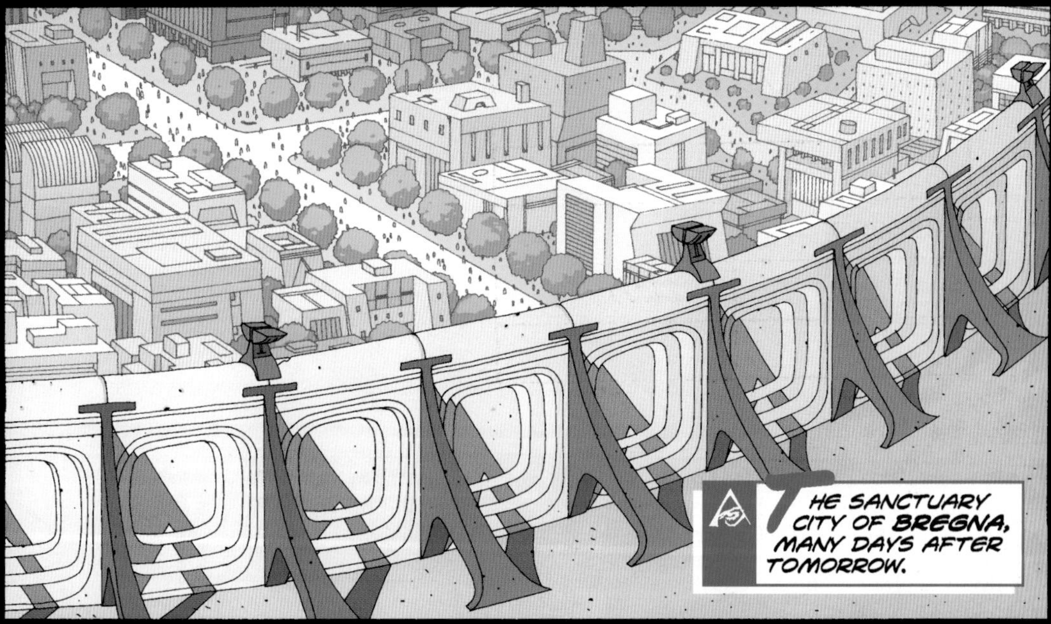
THE SANCTUARY CITY OF BREGNA, MANY DAYS AFTER TOMORROW.

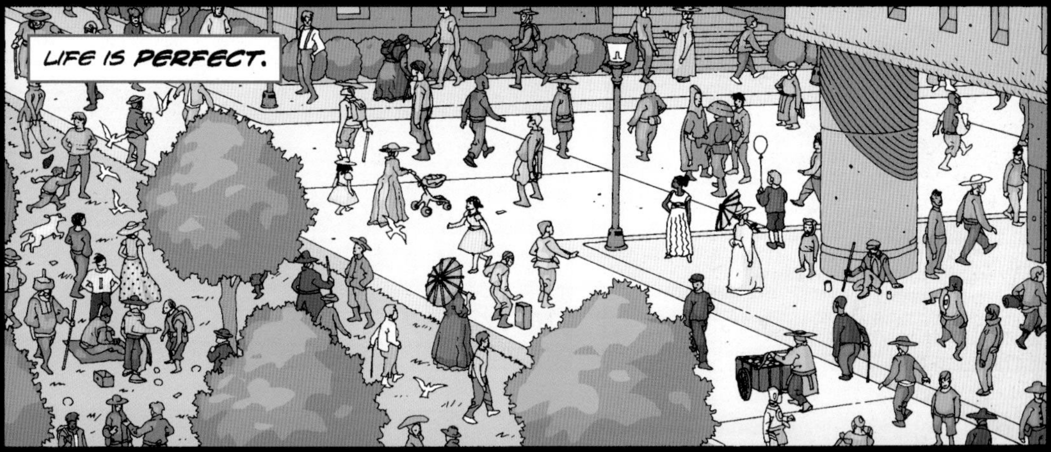
LIFE IS PERFECT.

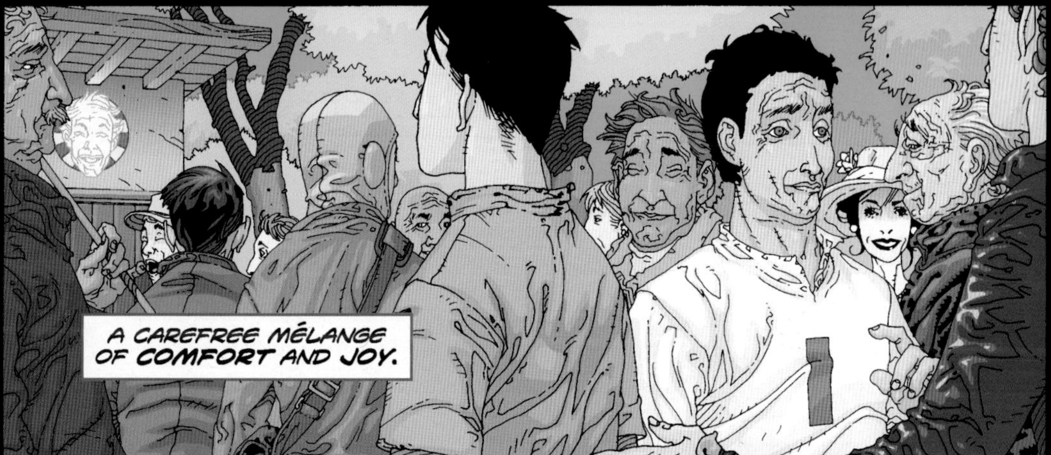
A CAREFREE MÉLANGE OF COMFORT AND JOY.

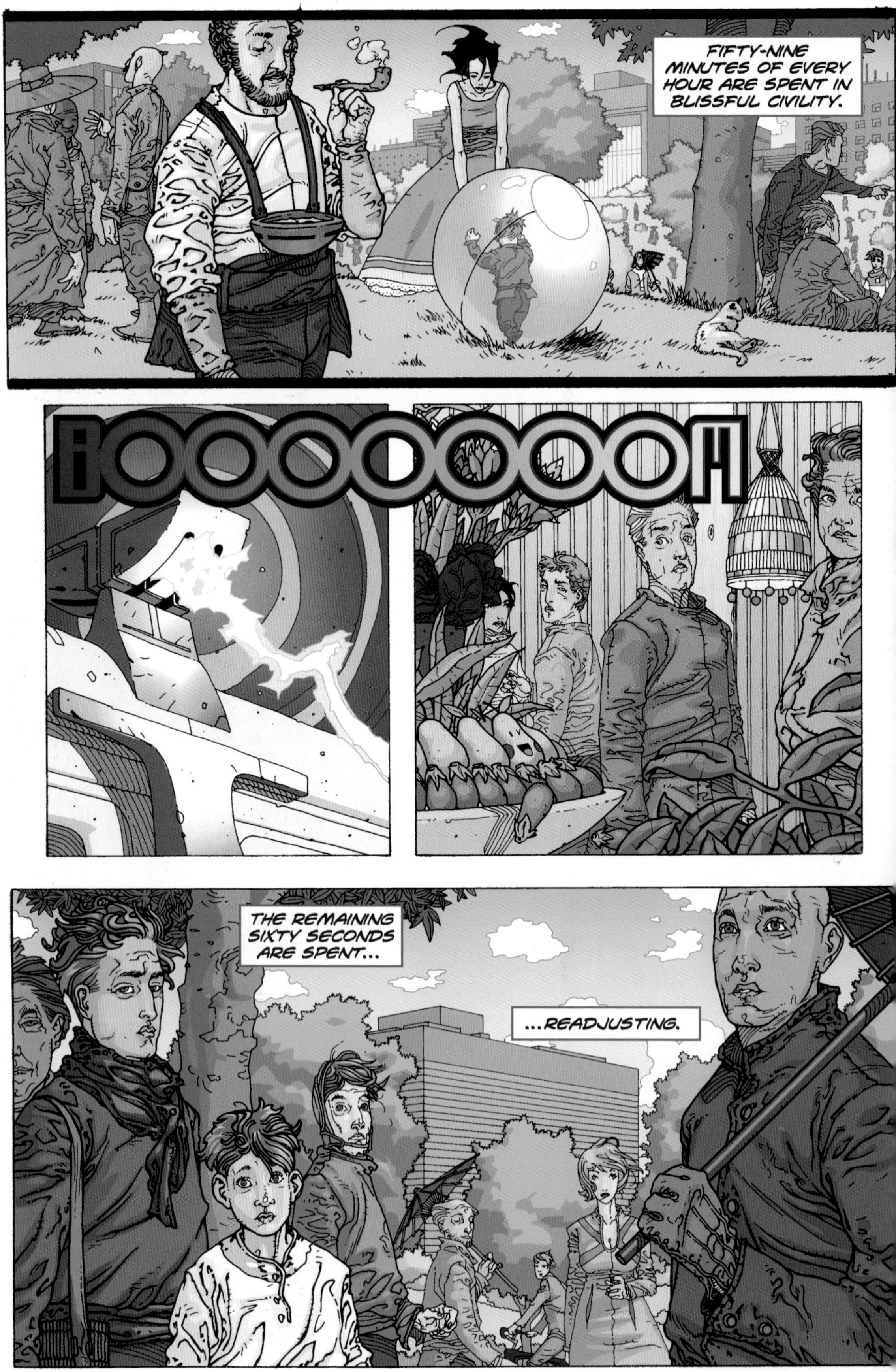
FIFTY-NINE MINUTES OF EVERY HOUR ARE SPENT IN BLISSFUL CIVILITY.
BOOOOOOOM
THE REMAINING SIXTY SECONDS ARE SPENT...
...READJUSTING.

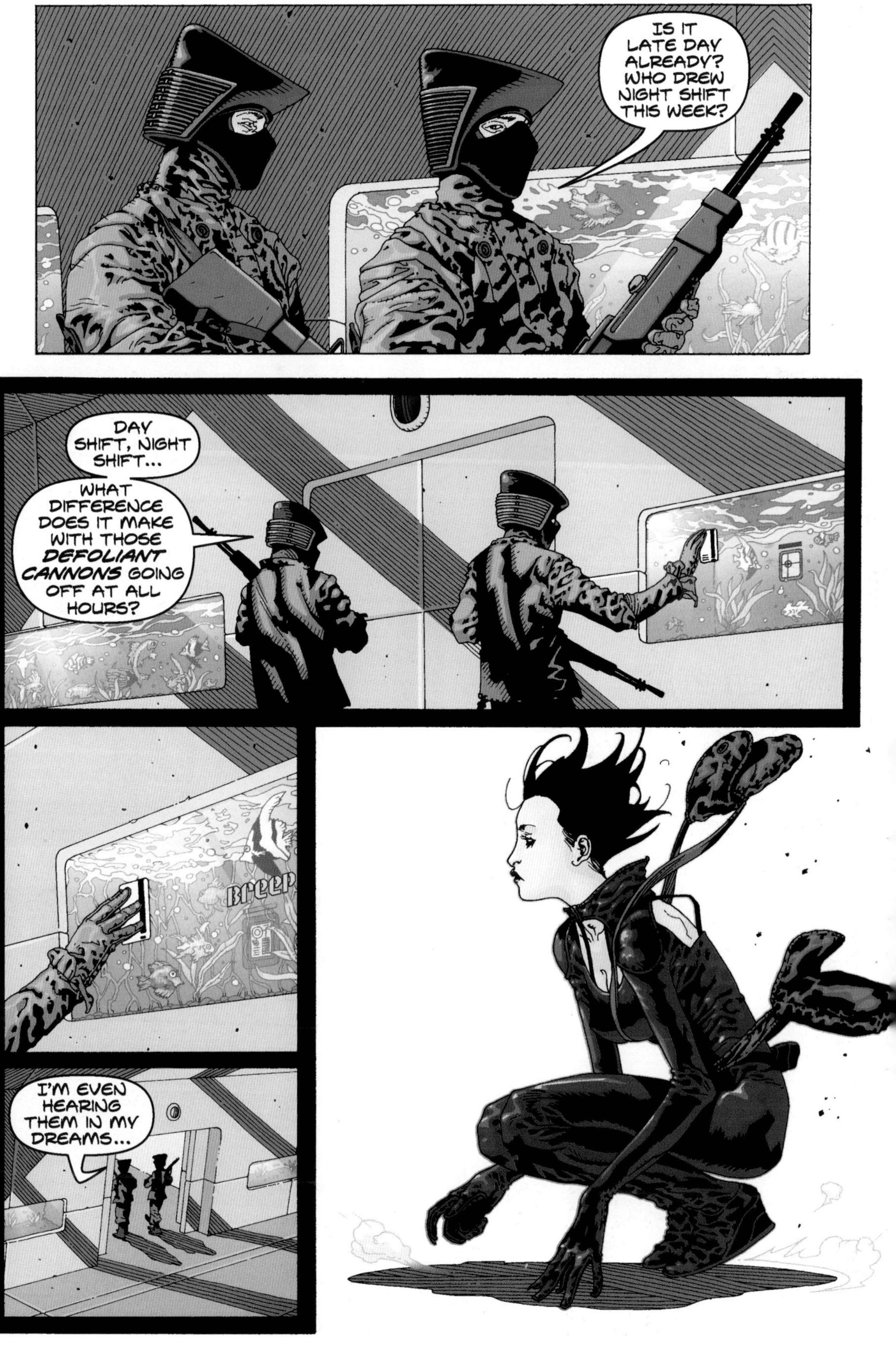
IS IT LATE DAY ALREADY? WHO DREW NIGHT SHIFT THIS WEEK?
DAY SHIFT, NIGHT SHIFT...
WHAT DIFFERENCE DOES IT MAKE WITH THOSE DEFOLIANT CANNONS GOING OFF AT ALL HOURS?
BREEP
I'M EVEN HEARING THEM IN MY DREAMS...

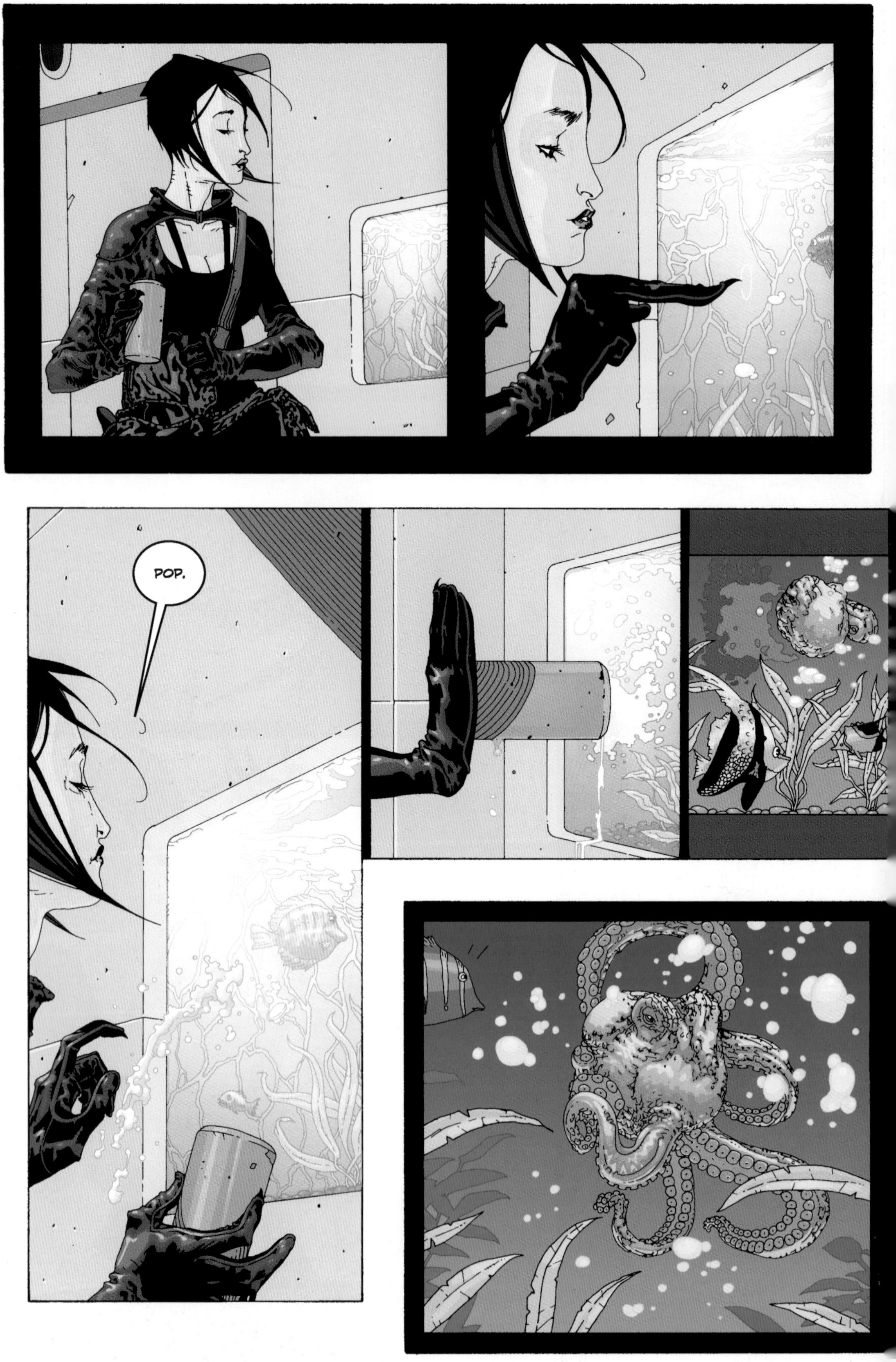
POP.

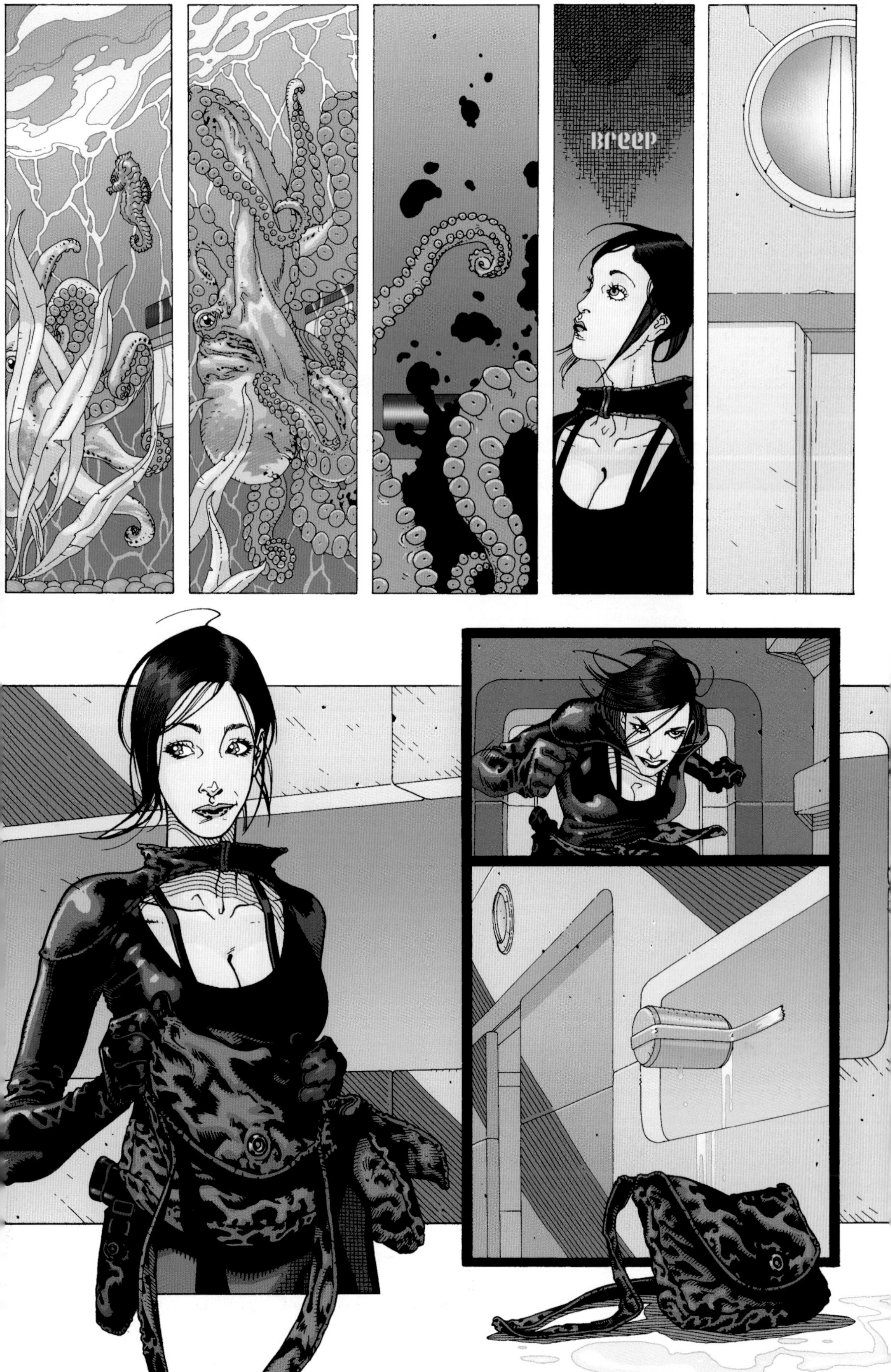
BREEP

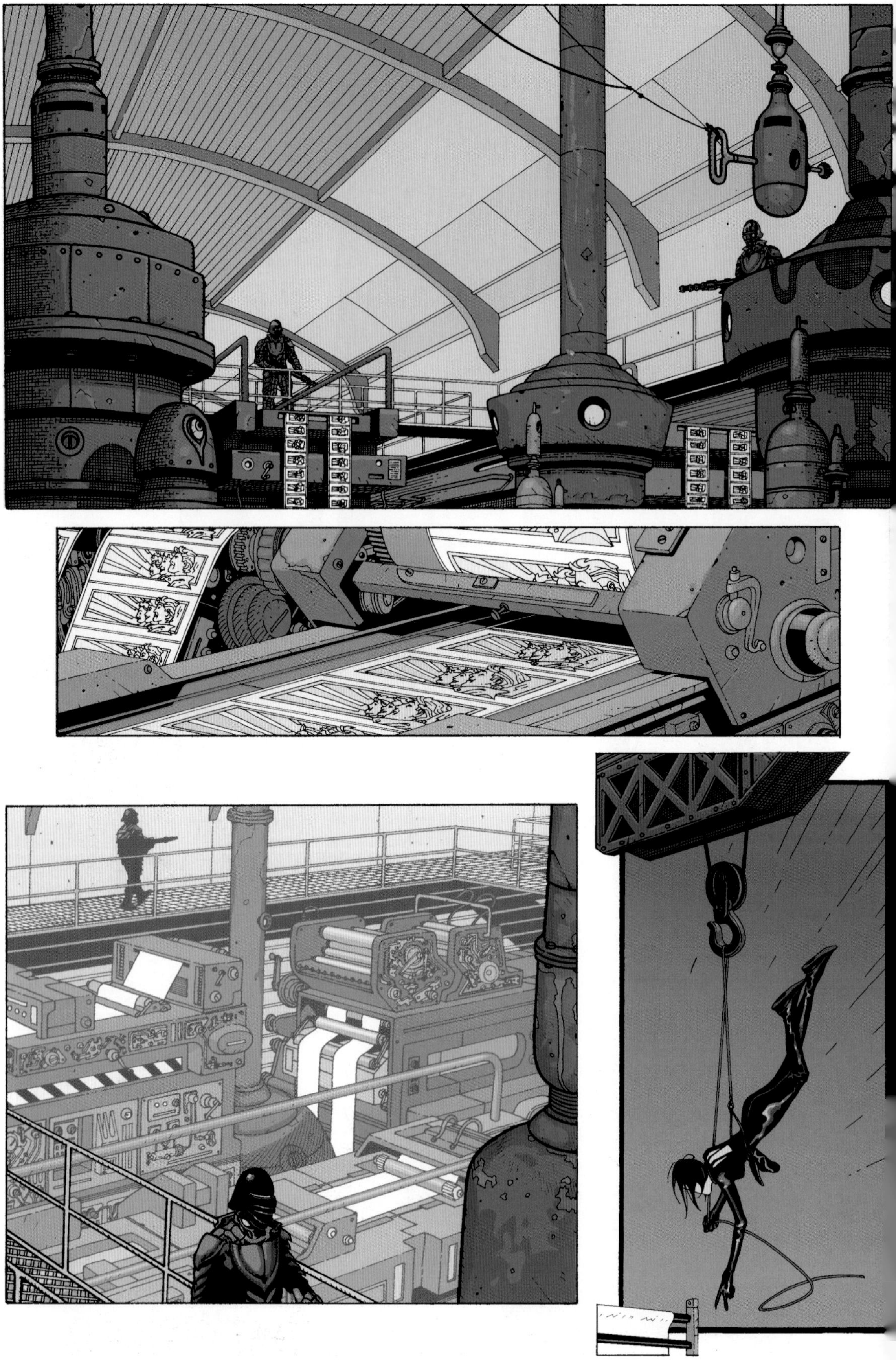

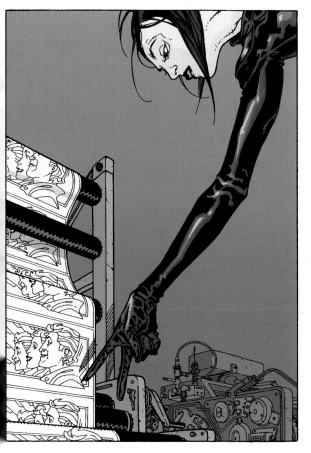

SNIP.

WEEEEEEENNNNNNCH-CHK-CHAAAAAK-K-K-K-KKK-

SABOTEUR!! STOP HER--!
BRAAA-A-A-APP!!

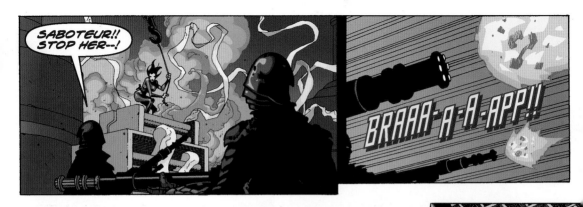

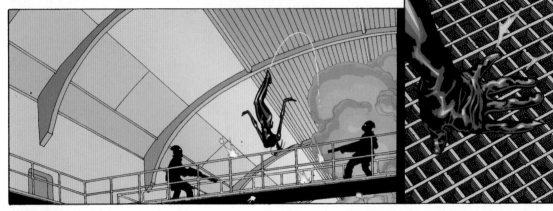

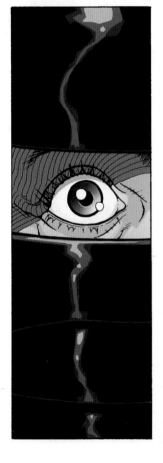

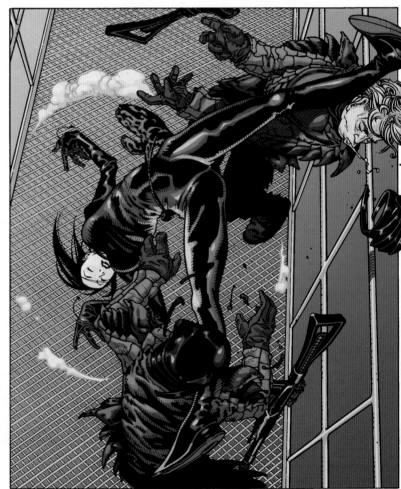

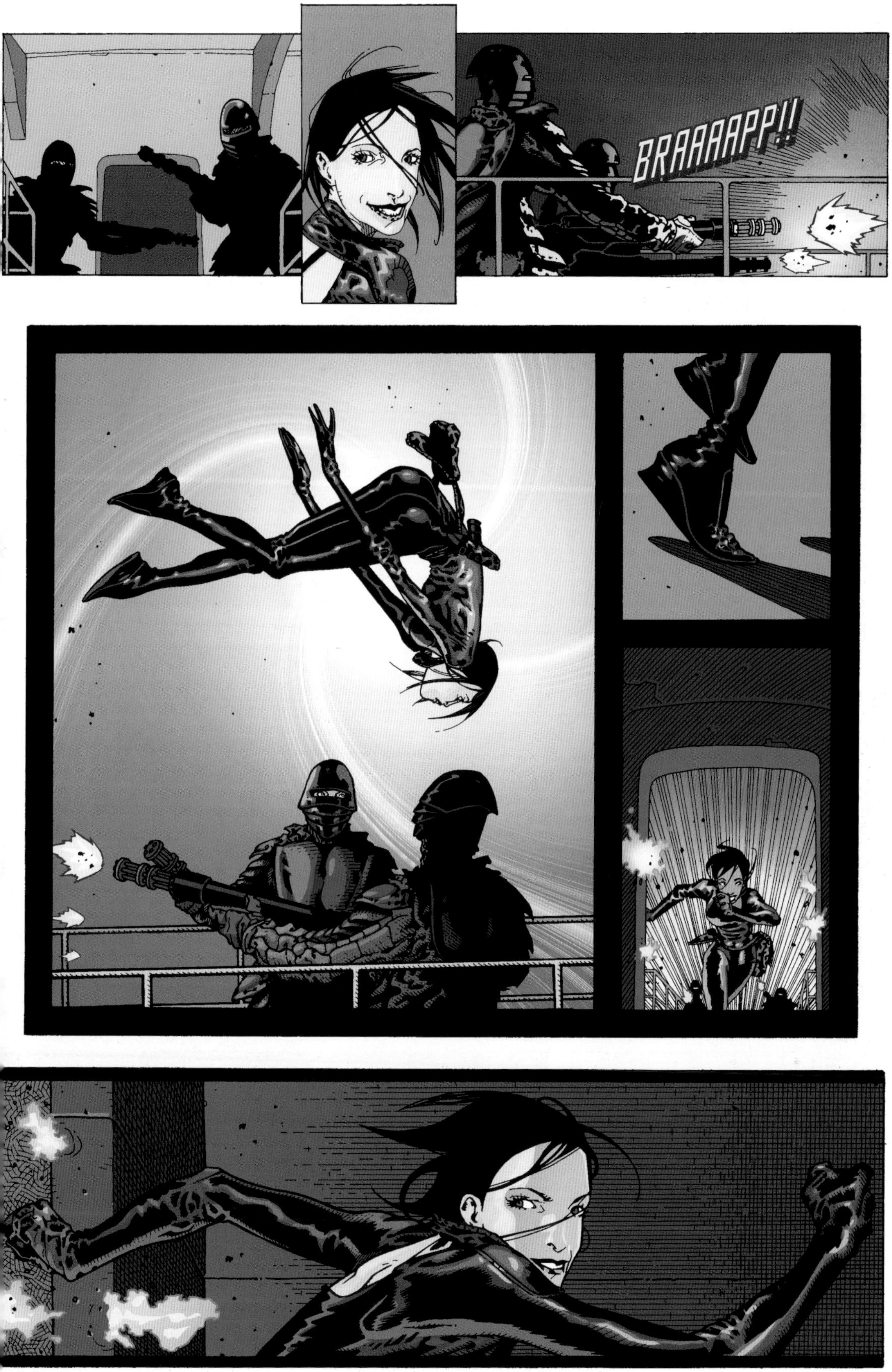
BRAAAAPP!!

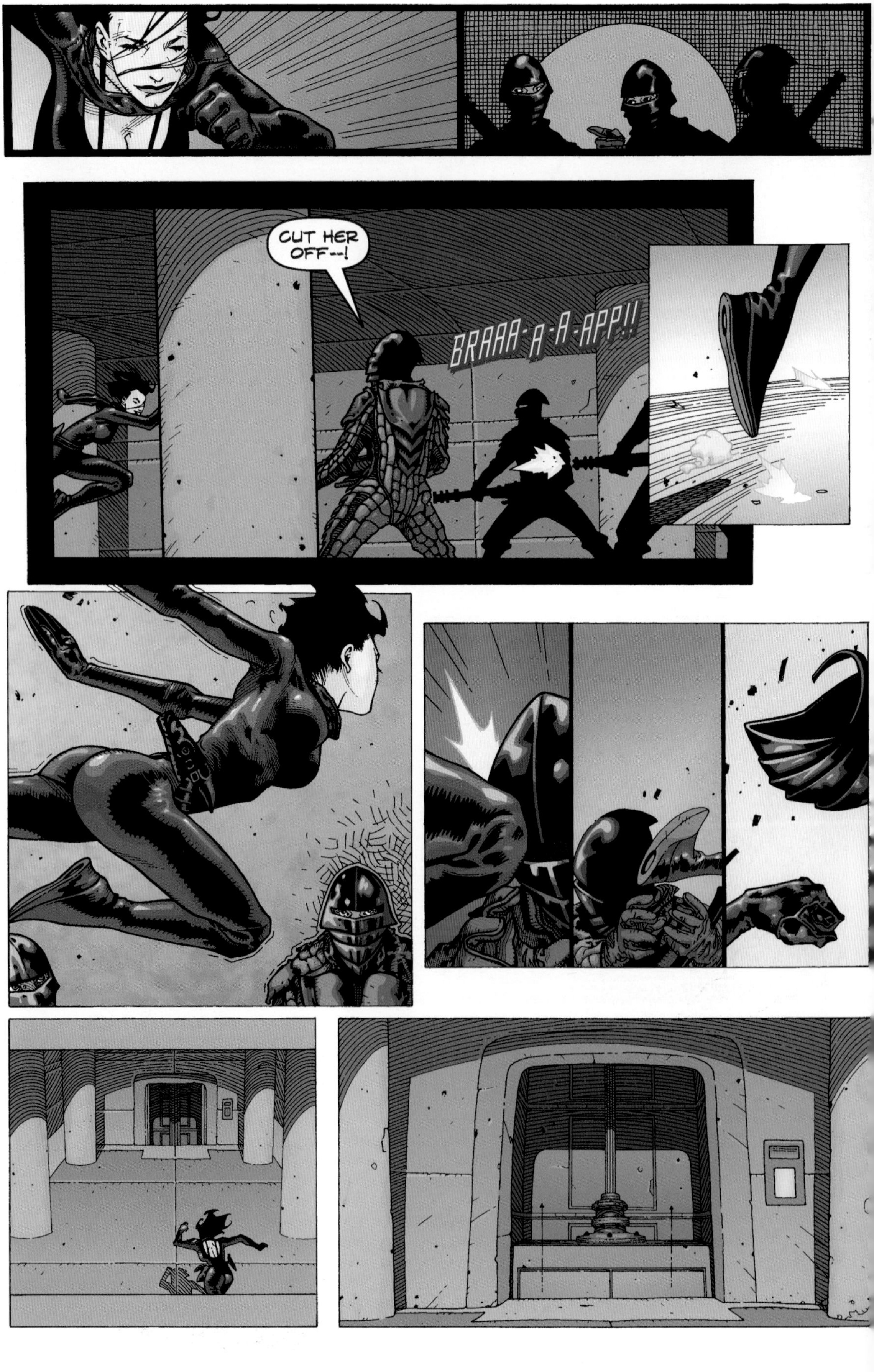
CUT HER OFF--!
BRAAA-A-A-APP!!

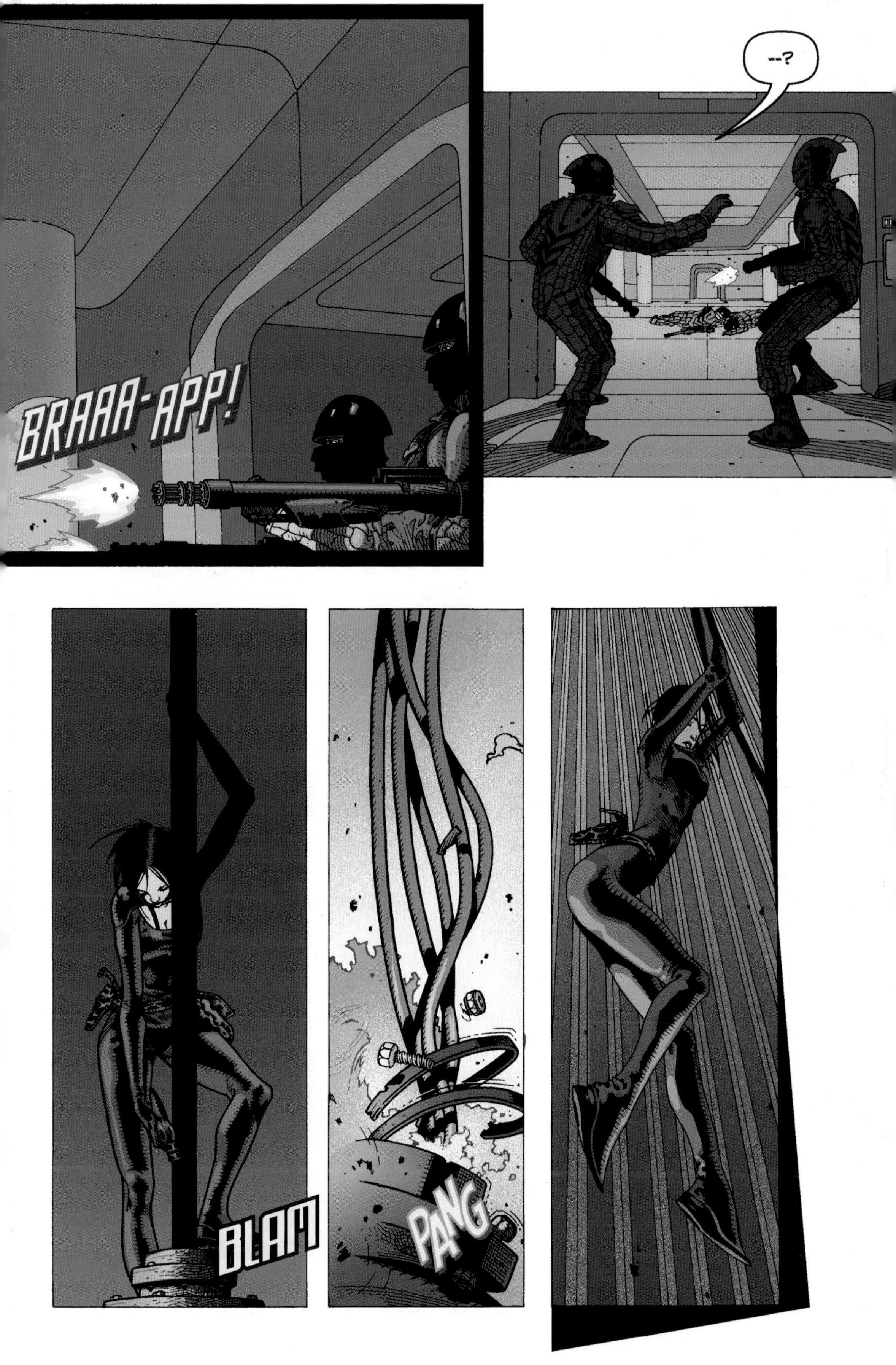
BRAAA-APP!
--?
BLAM
PANG

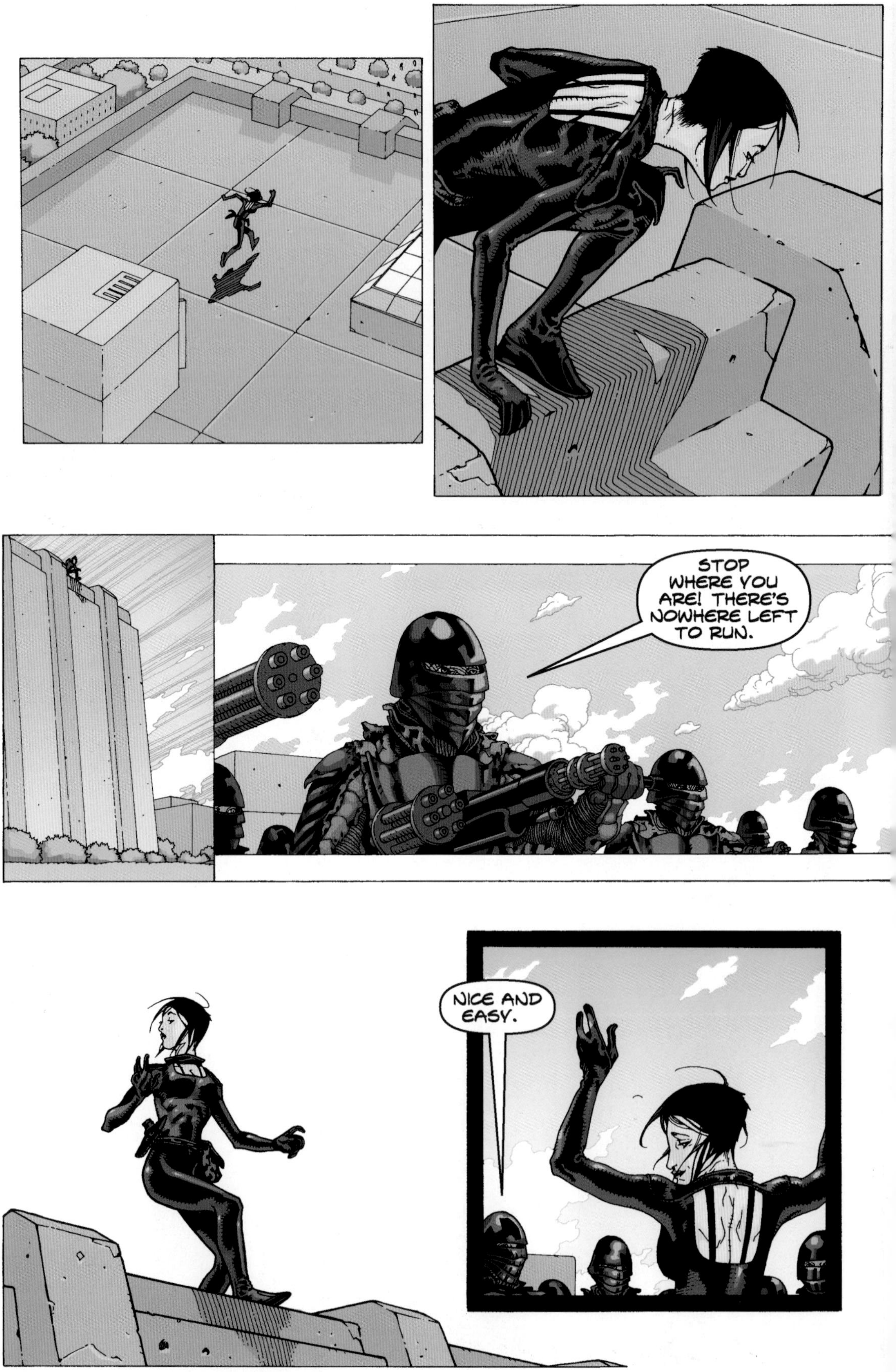
STOP WHERE YOU ARE! THERE'S NOWHERE LEFT TO RUN.
NICE AND EASY.

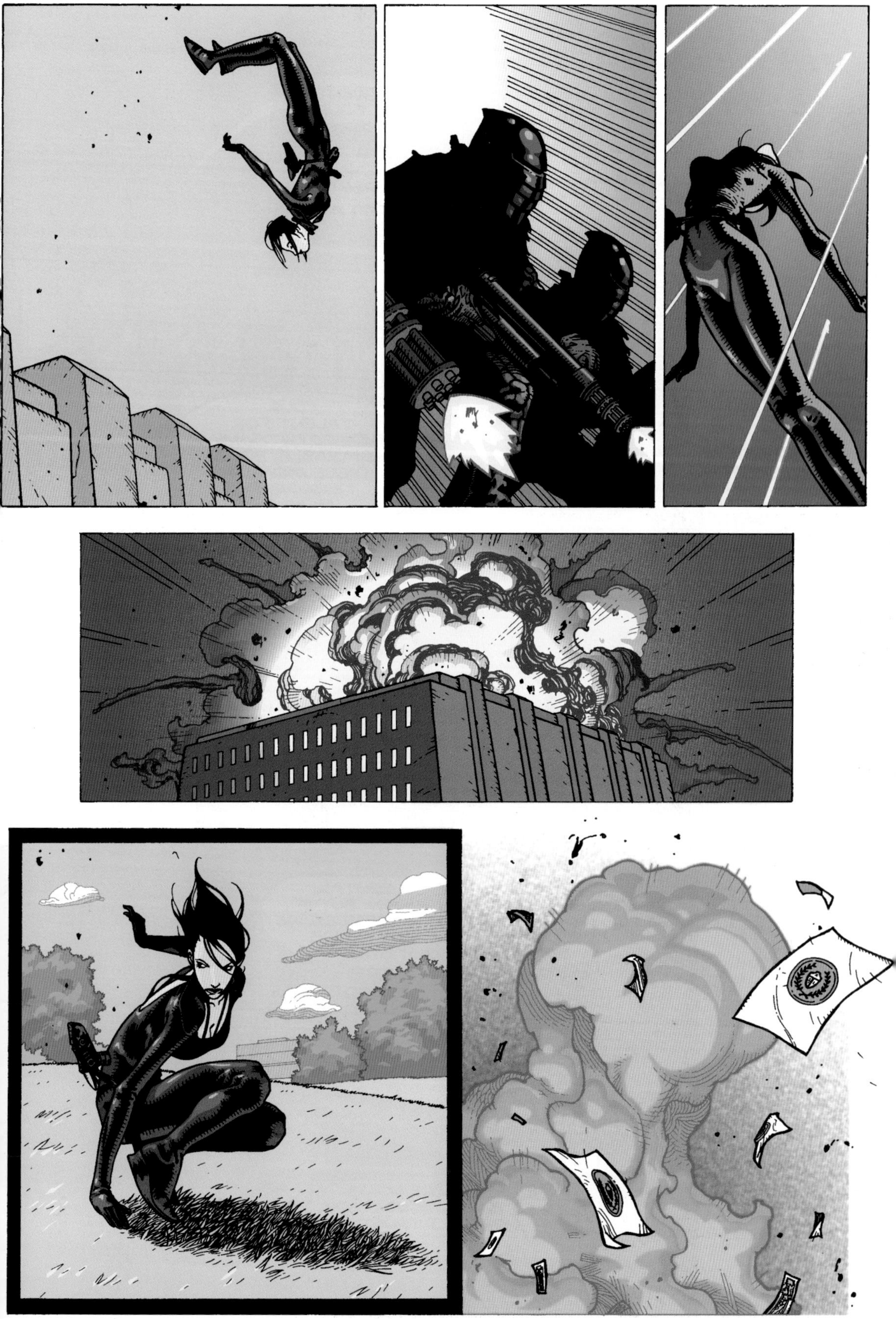

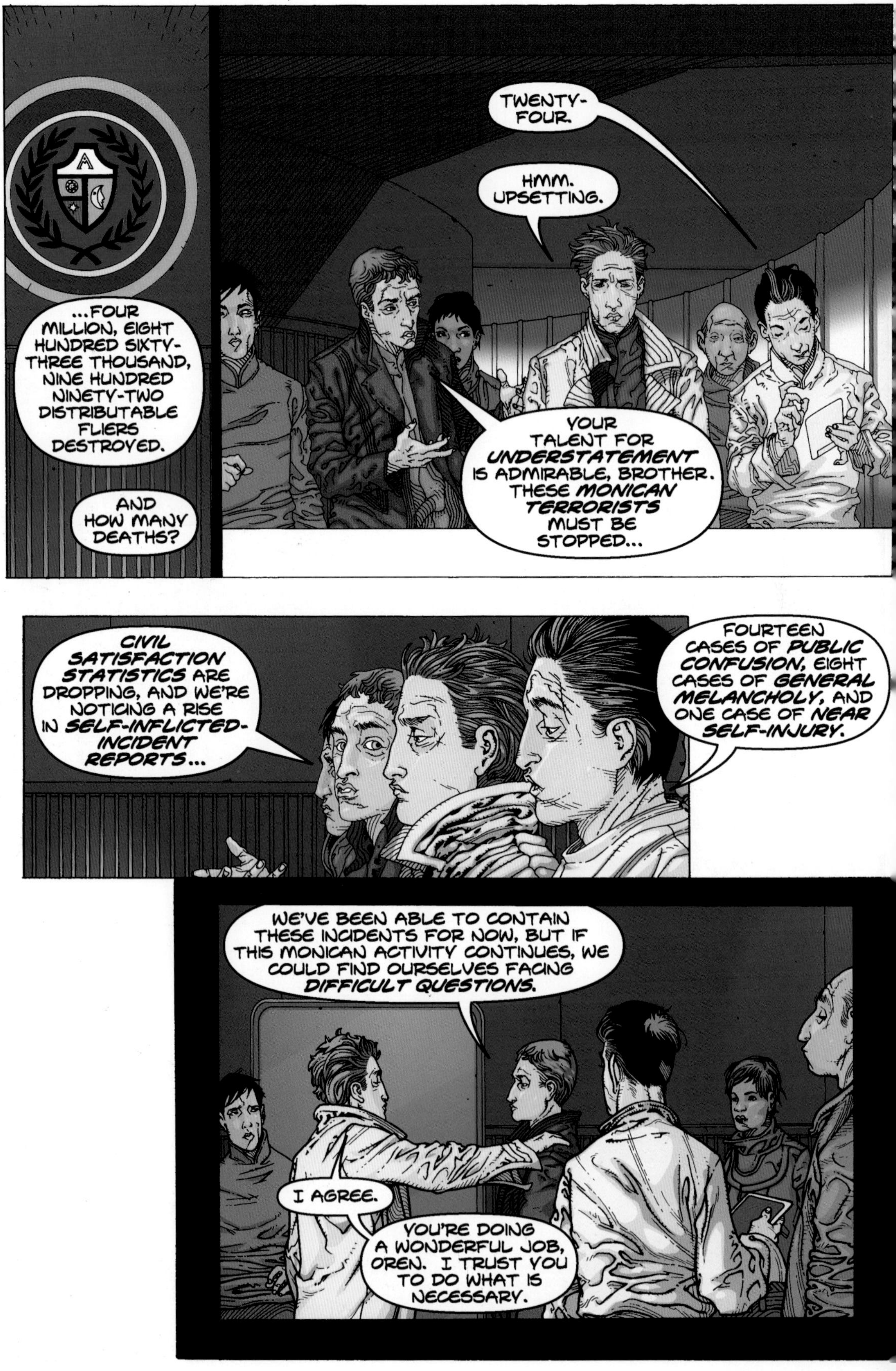
...FOUR MILLION, EIGHT HUNDRED SIXTY-THREE THOUSAND, NINE HUNDRED NINETY-TWO DISTRIBUTABLE FLIERS DESTROYED.
AND HOW MANY DEATHS?
TWENTY-FOUR.
HMM. UPSETTING.
YOUR TALENT FOR UNDERSTATEMENT IS ADMIRABLE, BROTHER. THESE MONICAN TERRORISTS MUST BE STOPPED...
CIVIL SATISFACTION STATISTICS ARE DROPPING, AND WE'RE NOTICING A RISE IN SELF-INFLICTED-INCIDENT REPORTS...
FOURTEEN CASES OF PUBLIC CONFUSION, EIGHT CASES OF GENERAL MELANCHOLY, AND ONE CASE OF NEAR SELF-INJURY.
WE'VE BEEN ABLE TO CONTAIN THESE INCIDENTS FOR NOW, BUT IF THIS MONICAN ACTIVITY CONTINUES, WE COULD FIND OURSELVES FACING DIFFICULT QUESTIONS.
I AGREE.
YOU'RE DOING A WONDERFUL JOB, OREN. I TRUST YOU TO DO WHAT IS NECESSARY.

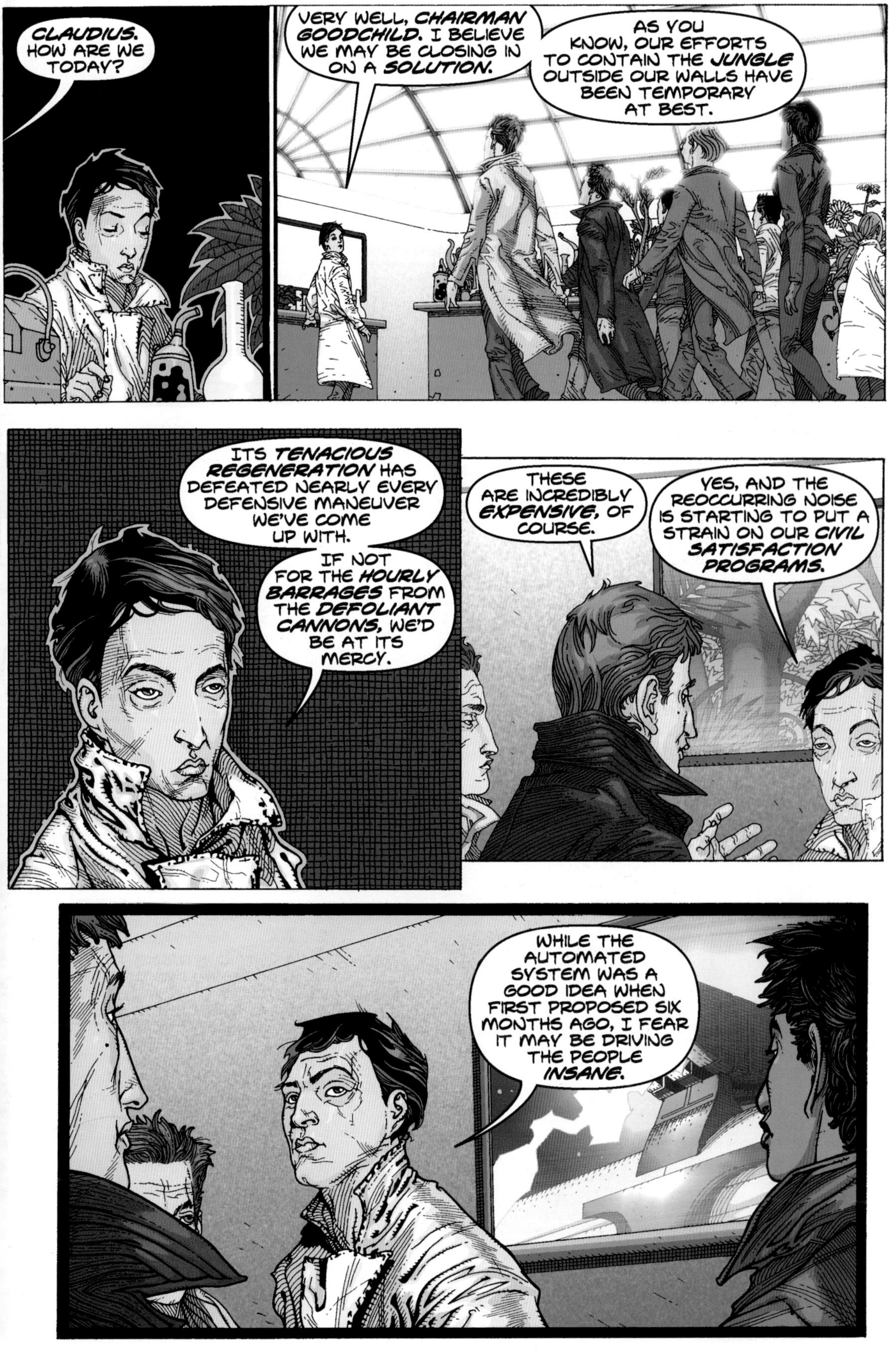
CLAUDIUS. HOW ARE WE TODAY?
VERY WELL, CHAIRMAN GOODCHILD. I BELIEVE WE MAY BE CLOSING IN ON A SOLUTION.
AS YOU KNOW, OUR EFFORTS TO CONTAIN THE JUNGLE OUTSIDE OUR WALLS HAVE BEEN TEMPORARY AT BEST.
ITS TENACIOUS REGENERATION HAS DEFEATED NEARLY EVERY DEFENSIVE MANEUVER WE'VE COME UP WITH.
IF NOT FOR THE HOURLY BARRAGES FROM THE DEFOLIANT CANNONS, WE'D BE AT ITS MERCY.
THESE ARE INCREDIBLY EXPENSIVE, OF COURSE.
YES, AND THE REOCCURRING NOISE IS STARTING TO PUT A STRAIN ON OUR CIVIL SATISFACTION PROGRAMS.
WHILE THE AUTOMATED SYSTEM WAS A GOOD IDEA WHEN FIRST PROPOSED SIX MONTHS AGO, I FEAR IT MAY BE DRIVING THE PEOPLE INSANE.

BUT I'M HAPPY TO ANNOUNCE WE MAY HAVE FINALLY DEVELOPED A CHEMICAL DEFOLIANT STRONG ENOUGH TO DESTROY THE JUNGLE ONCE AND FOR ALL.
THAT'S VERY GOOD NEWS.
"GOOD," INDEED.
BY ATTACKING ALL FORMS OF RNA, IT WILL PREVENT ANY CELLULAR MESSAGE FROM INITIATING REGENERATION OR REPRO-DUCTION.
WE NEUTER IT, AND THEN WE KILL IT.
WE'VE BEEN CALLING IT "OMNIMATRI-CIDE."
"--MATRICIDE"...?
WE SHOULD BEGIN PRACTICAL APPLICATION IMMEDIATELY. THE SOONER WE END THIS THREAT, THE SOONER WE CAN START EXTENDING THE WALLS...
ER, YES, BUT... WELL, RESULTS HAVE BEEN PROMISING, BUT WE STILL HAVE MANY TESTS TO RUN. I FEAR THIS CHEMICAL MIGHT WORK TOO WELL.
IT'S POSSIBLE THAT IT COULD DESTROY EVERY BIT OF ORGANIC MATTER IT TOUCHES, LEAVING THE EARTH IRONICALLY BARREN AS A RESULT...
I'D LIKE TO TAILOR THE DEFOLIANT TO ONLY TARGET THOSE AGGRESSIVE SPECIES CAUSING MOST OF OUR TROUBLE...

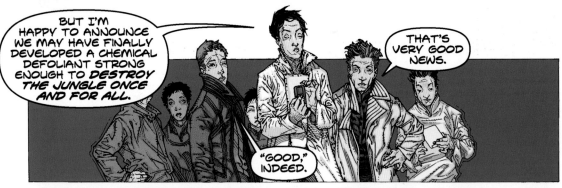

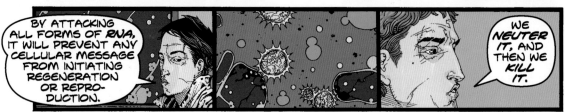

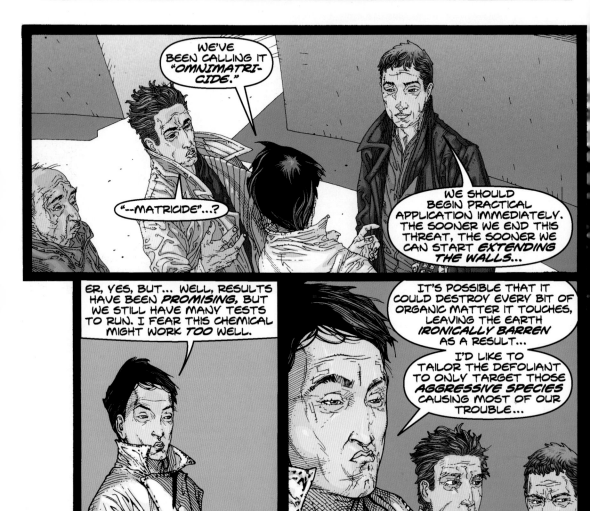

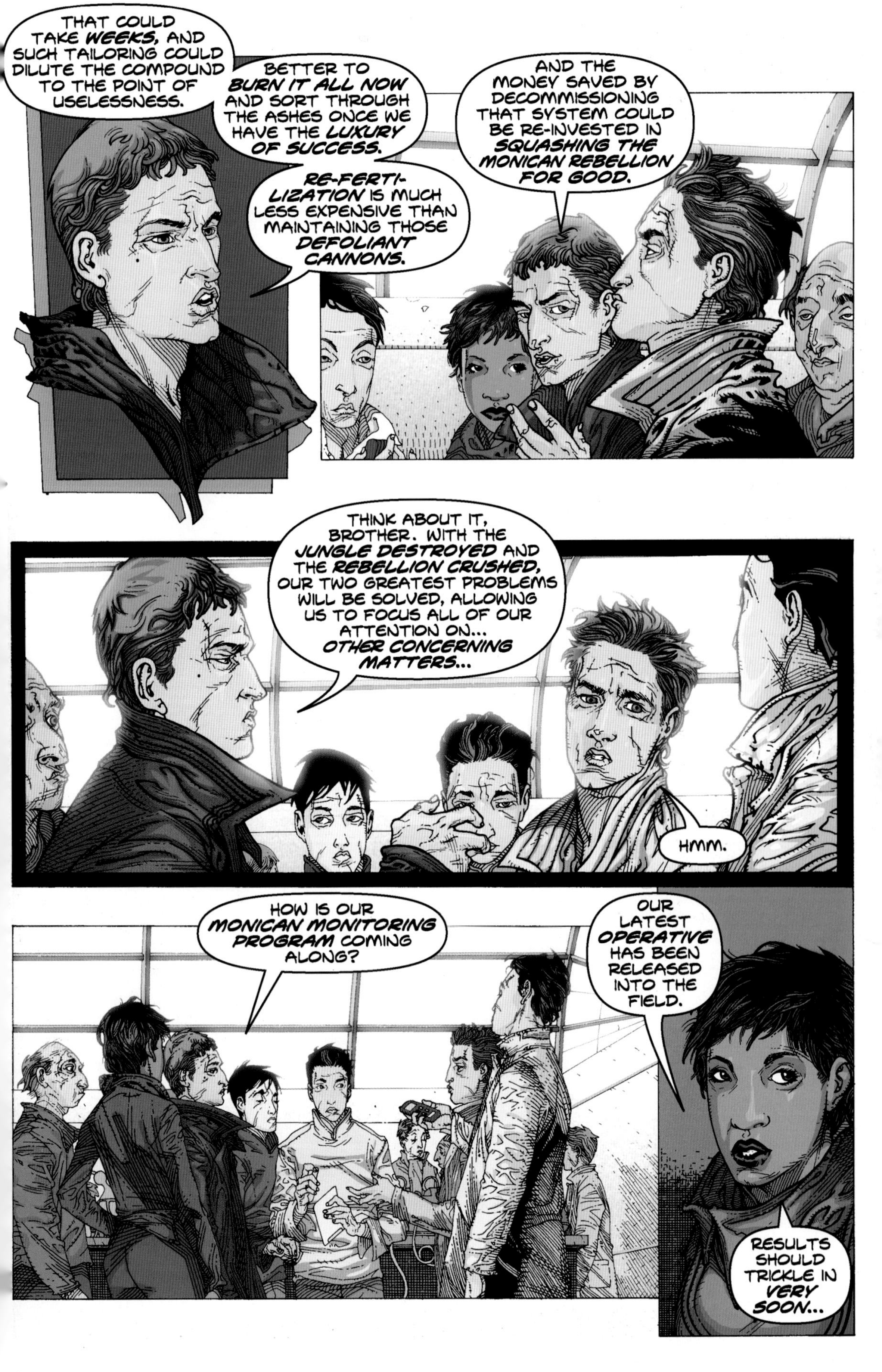
THAT COULD TAKE WEEKS, AND SUCH TAILORING COULD DILUTE THE COMPOUND TO THE POINT OF USELESSNESS.
BETTER TO BURN IT ALL NOW AND SORT THROUGH THE ASHES ONCE WE HAVE THE LUXURY OF SUCCESS.
RE-FERTILIZATION IS MUCH LESS EXPENSIVE THAN MAINTAINING THOSE DEFOLIANT CANNONS.
AND THE MONEY SAVED BY DECOMMISSIONING THAT SYSTEM COULD BE RE-INVESTED IN SQUASHING THE MONICAN REBELLION FOR GOOD.
THINK ABOUT IT, BROTHER. WITH THE JUNGLE DESTROYED AND THE REBELLION CRUSHED, OUR TWO GREATEST PROBLEMS WILL BE SOLVED, ALLOWING US TO FOCUS ALL OF OUR ATTENTION ON... OTHER CONCERNING MATTERS...
HMM.
HOW IS OUR MONICAN MONITORING PROGRAM COMING ALONG?
OUR LATEST OPERATIVE HAS BEEN RELEASED INTO THE FIELD.
RESULTS SHOULD TRICKLE IN VERY SOON...

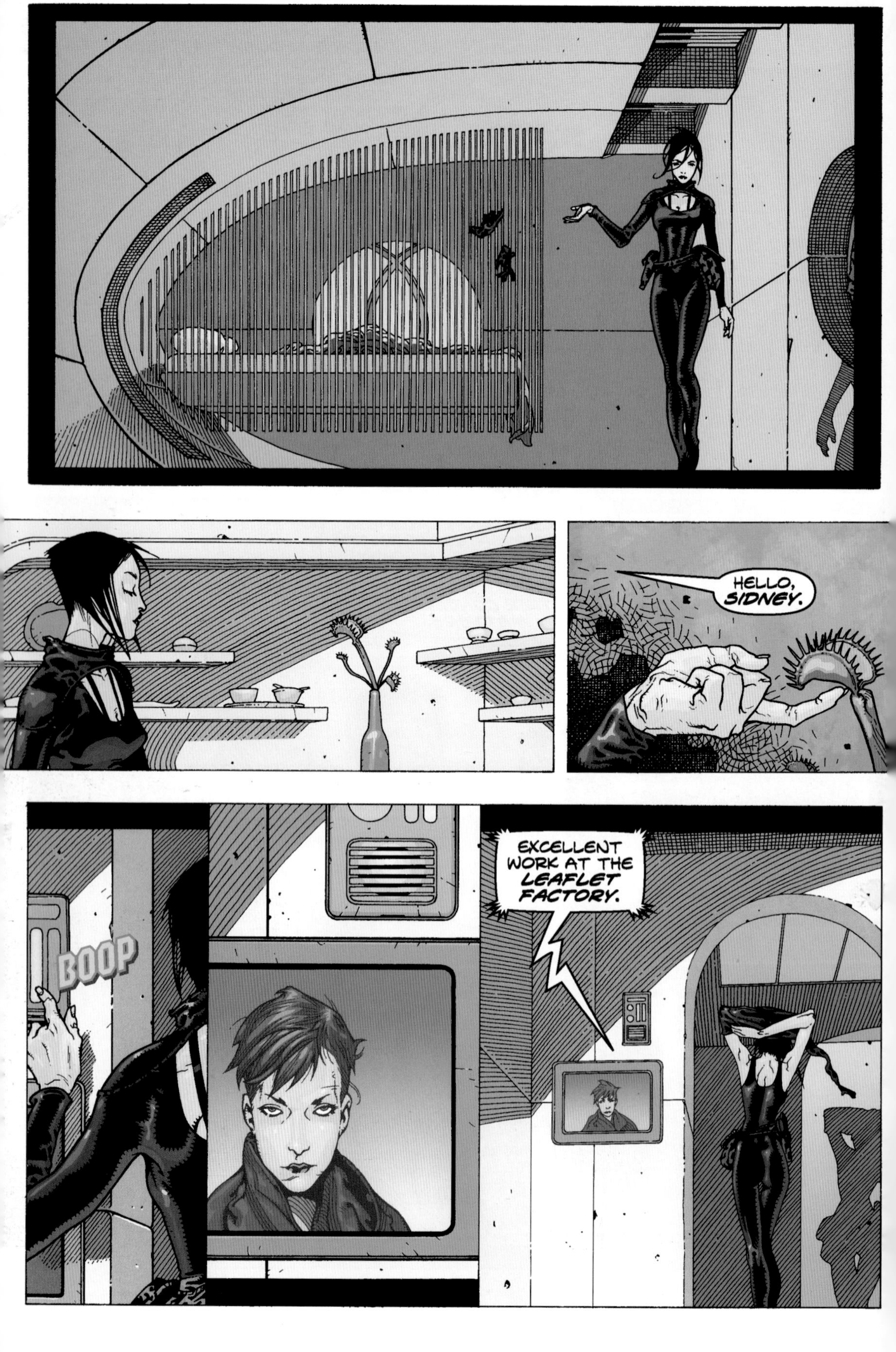
HELLO, SIDNEY.
BOOP
EXCELLENT WORK AT THE LEAFLET FACTORY.

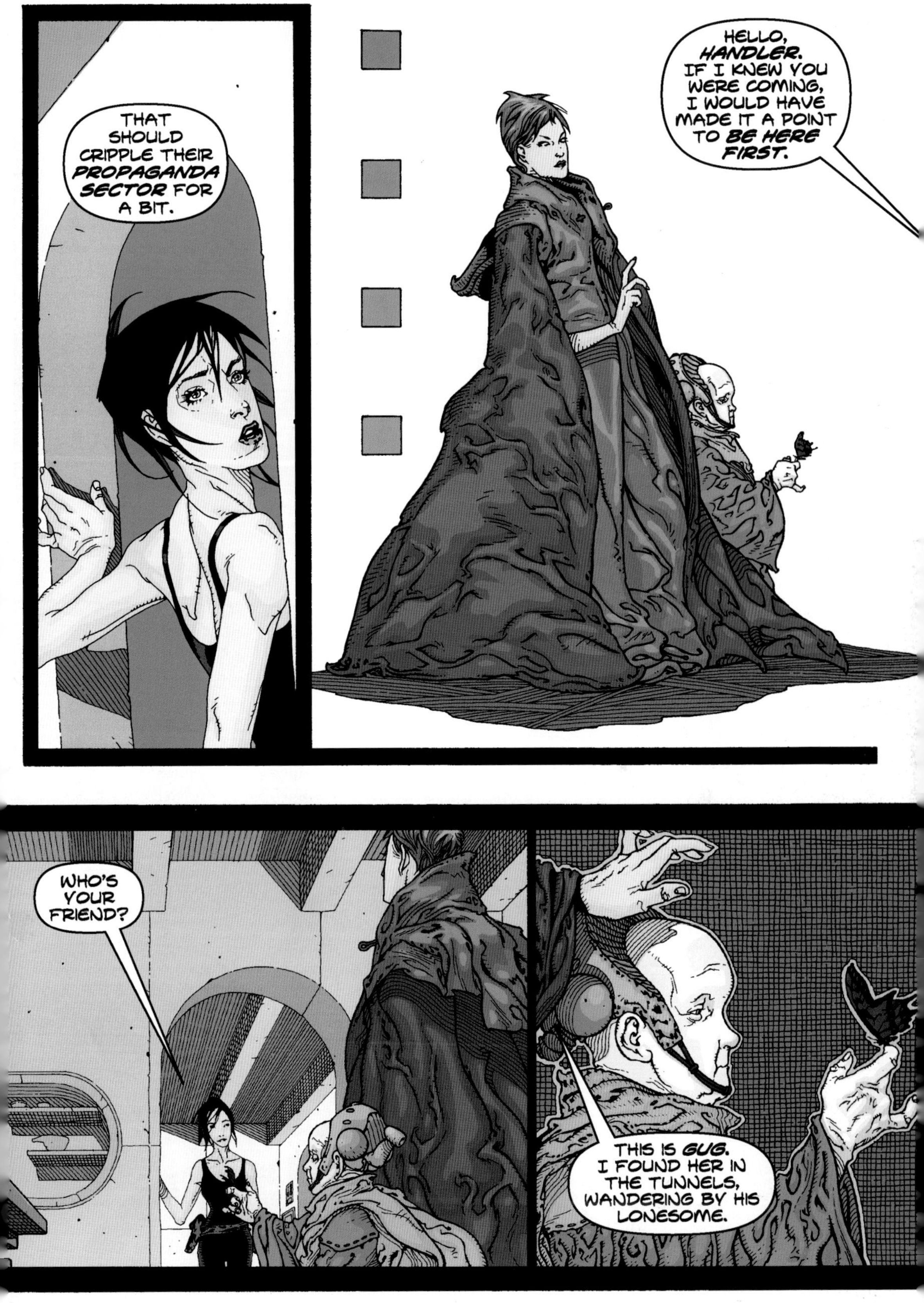
THAT SHOULD CRIPPLE THEIR PROPAGANDA SECTOR FOR A BIT.
HELLO, HANDLER. IF I KNEW YOU WERE COMING, I WOULD HAVE MADE IT A POINT TO BE HERE FIRST.
WHO'S YOUR FRIEND?
THIS IS GUG. I FOUND HER IN THE TUNNELS, WANDERING BY HIS LONESOME.

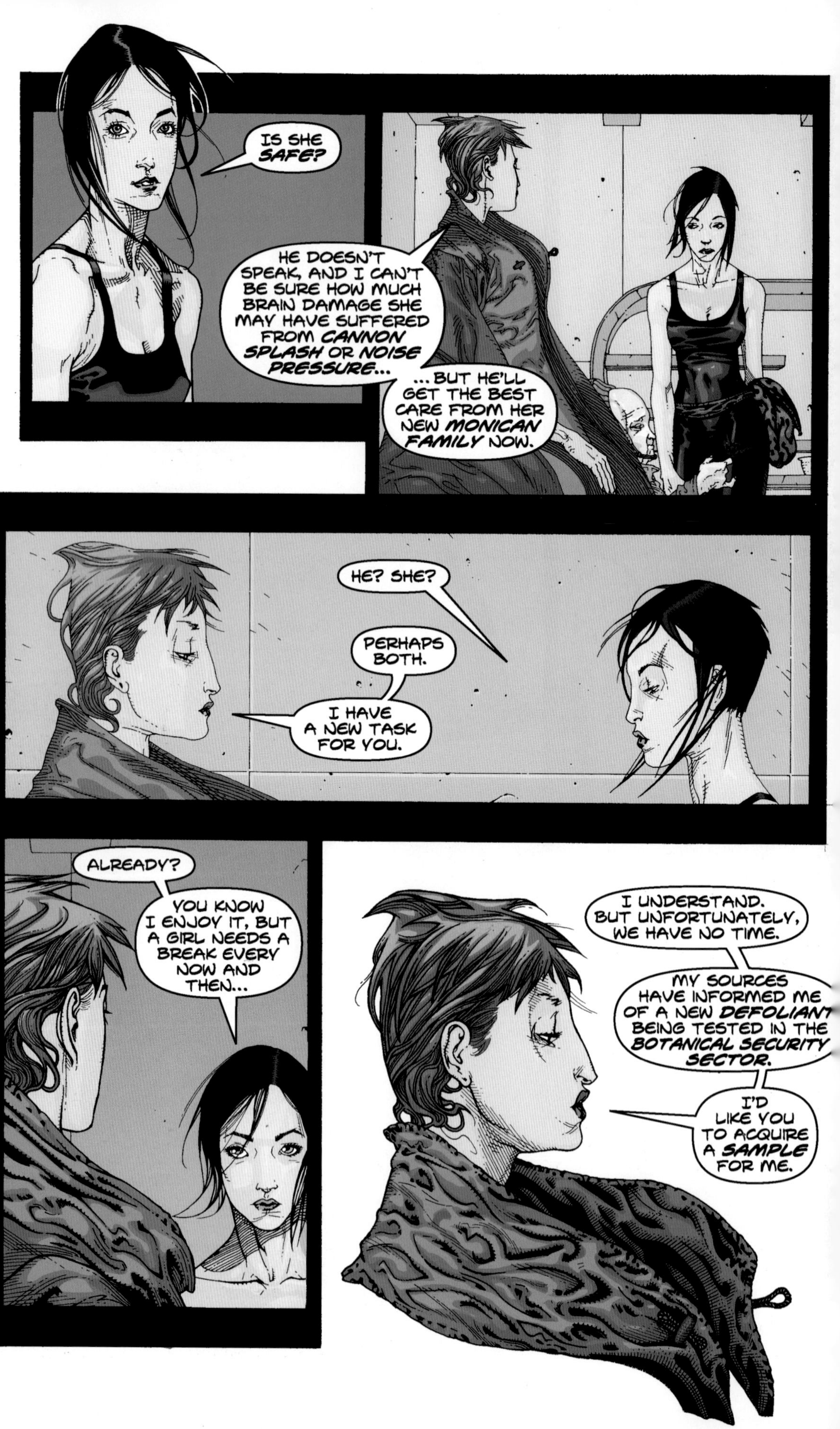
IS SHE SAFE?
HE DOESN'T SPEAK, AND I CAN'T BE SURE HOW MUCH BRAIN DAMAGE SHE MAY HAVE SUFFERED FROM CANNON SPLASH OR NOISE PRESSURE...
...BUT HE'LL GET THE BEST CARE FROM HER NEW MONICAN FAMILY NOW.
HE? SHE?
PERHAPS BOTH.
I HAVE A NEW TASK FOR YOU.
ALREADY?
YOU KNOW I ENJOY IT, BUT A GIRL NEEDS A BREAK EVERY NOW AND THEN...
I UNDERSTAND. BUT UNFORTUNATELY, WE HAVE NO TIME.
MY SOURCES HAVE INFORMED ME OF A NEW DEFOLIANT BEING TESTED IN THE BOTANICAL SECURITY SECTOR.
I'D LIKE YOU TO ACQUIRE A SAMPLE FOR ME.

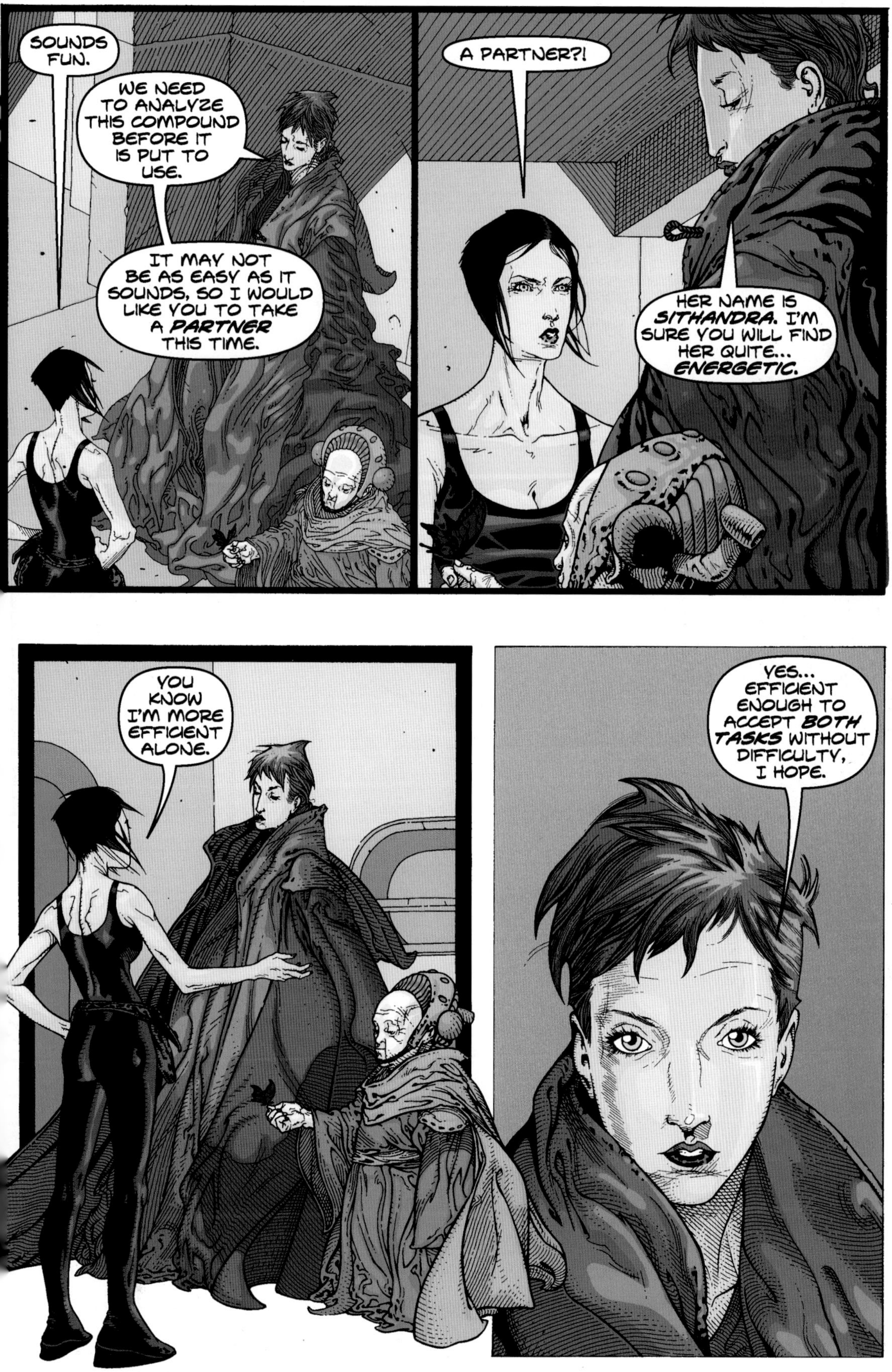
SOUNDS FUN.
WE NEED TO ANALYZE THIS COMPOUND BEFORE IT IS PUT TO USE.
IT MAY NOT BE AS EASY AS IT SOUNDS, SO I WOULD LIKE YOU TO TAKE A *PARTNER* THIS TIME.
A PARTNER?!
HER NAME IS *SITHANDRA*. I'M SURE YOU WILL FIND HER QUITE... *ENERGETIC*.
YOU KNOW I'M MORE EFFICIENT ALONE.
YES... EFFICIENT ENOUGH TO ACCEPT *BOTH TASKS* WITHOUT DIFFICULTY, I HOPE.

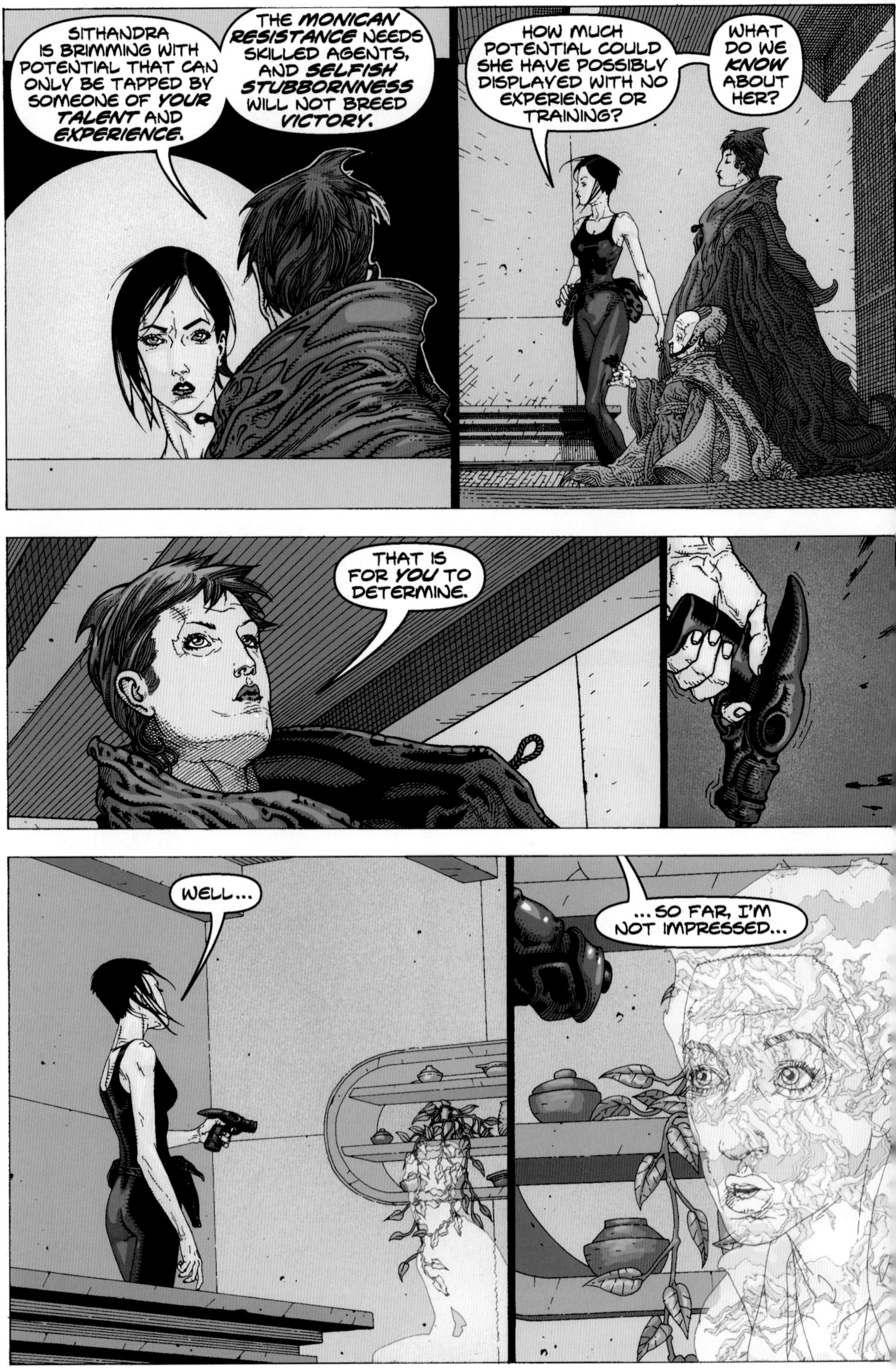
SITHANDRA IS BRIMMING WITH POTENTIAL THAT CAN ONLY BE TAPPED BY SOMEONE OF YOUR TALENT AND EXPERIENCE.
THE MONICAN RESISTANCE NEEDS SKILLED AGENTS, AND SELFISH STUBBORNNESS WILL NOT BREED VICTORY.
HOW MUCH POTENTIAL COULD SHE HAVE POSSIBLY DISPLAYED WITH NO EXPERIENCE OR TRAINING?
WHAT DO WE KNOW ABOUT HER?
THAT IS FOR YOU TO DETERMINE.
WELL...
...SO FAR, I'M NOT IMPRESSED...

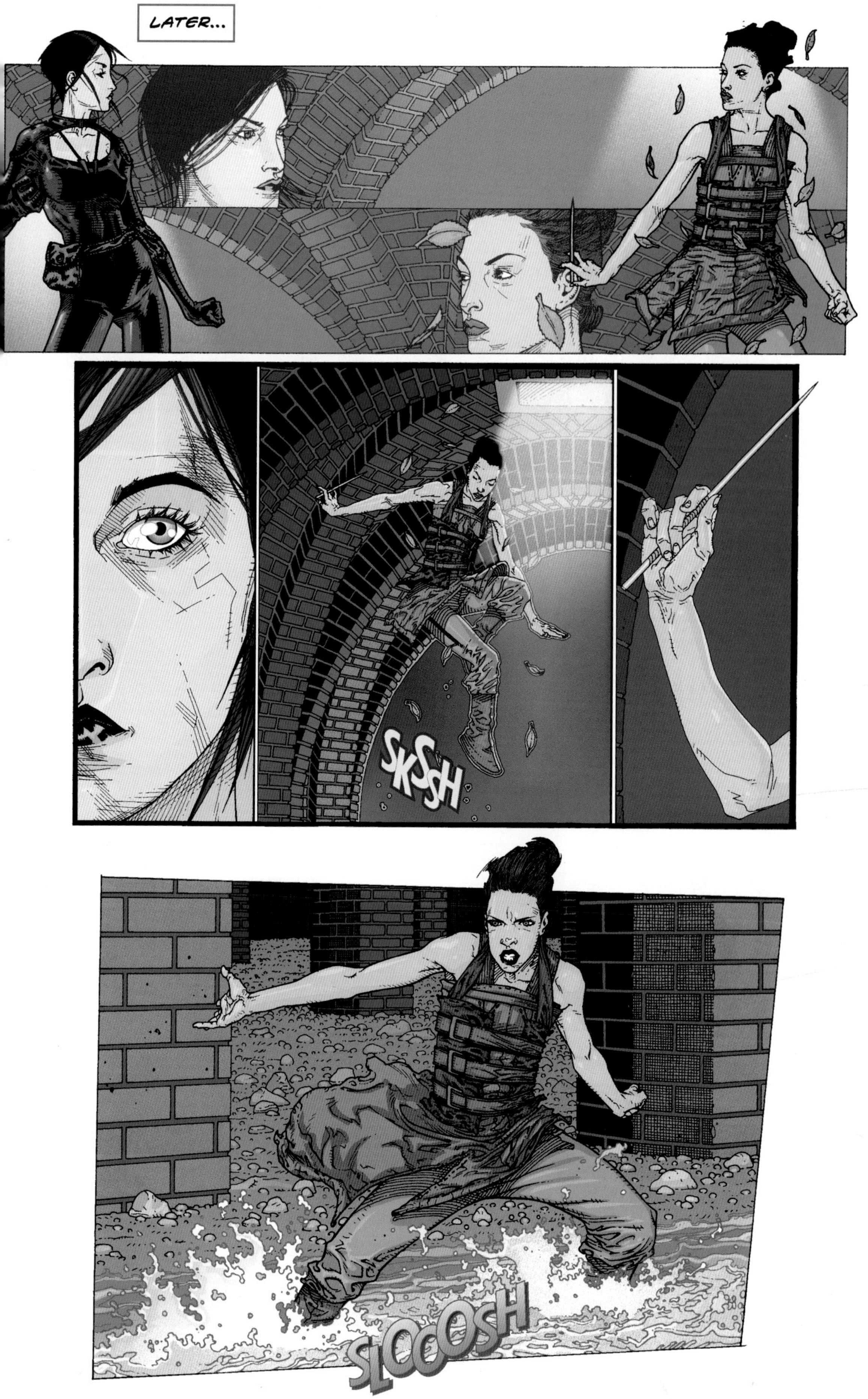
LATER...
SKSSH
SLOOOSH

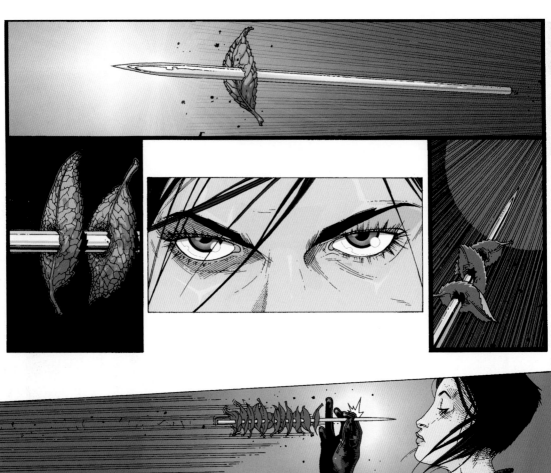

NOT BAD.

BUT NOT GOOD ENOUGH, IS THAT WHAT YOU'RE THINKING?

WE'RE WASTING TIME WHEN WE SHOULD BE PLANNING OUR MISSION.

THE MISSION IS PROCEEDING ON ITS OWN. I'LL DECIDE WHETHER YOU'LL SERVE ANY USEFUL PART IN IT.

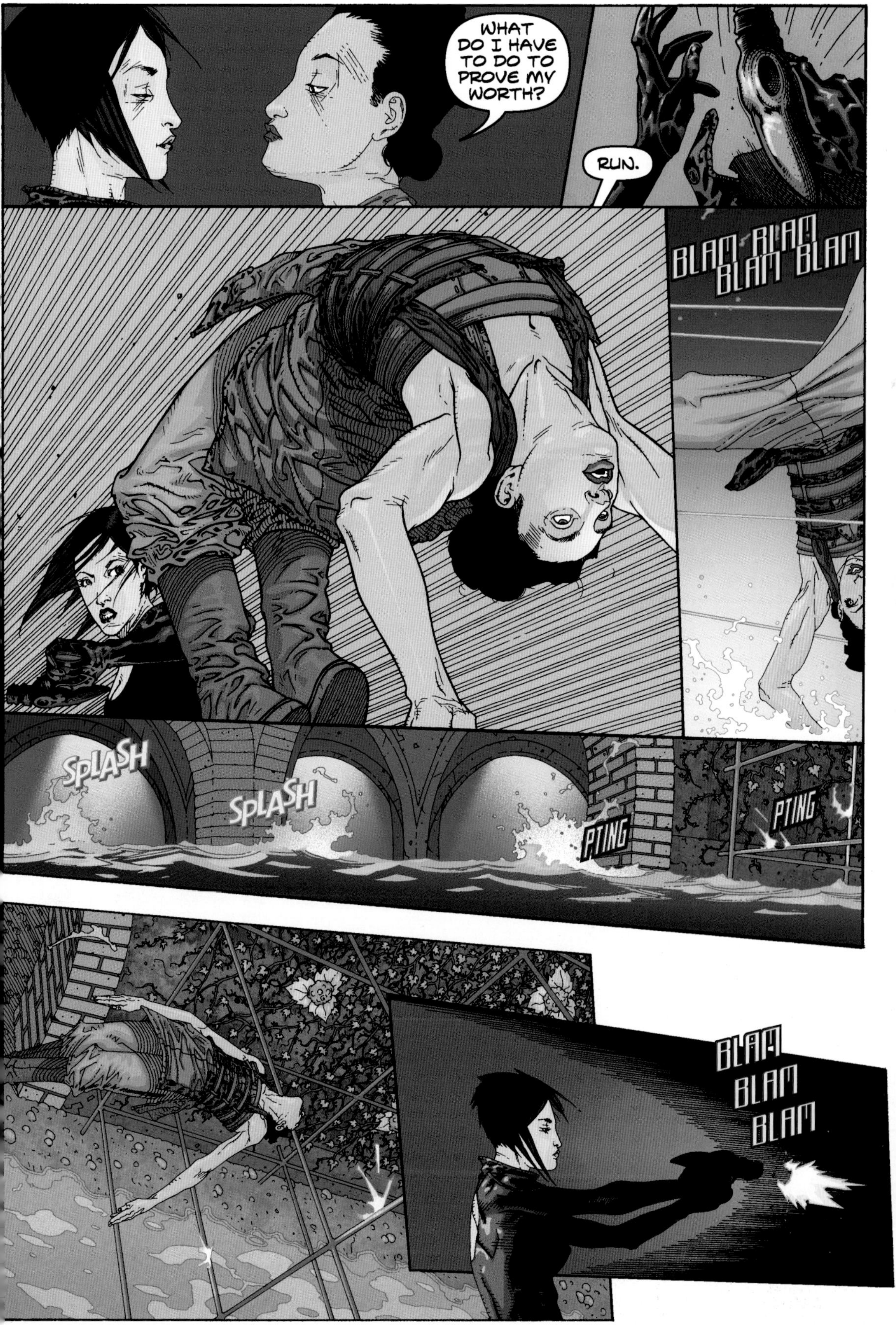
WHAT DO I HAVE TO DO TO PROVE MY WORTH?
RUN.
BLAM BLAM BLAM BLAM
SPLASH
SPLASH
PTING
PTING
BLAM
BLAM
BLAM

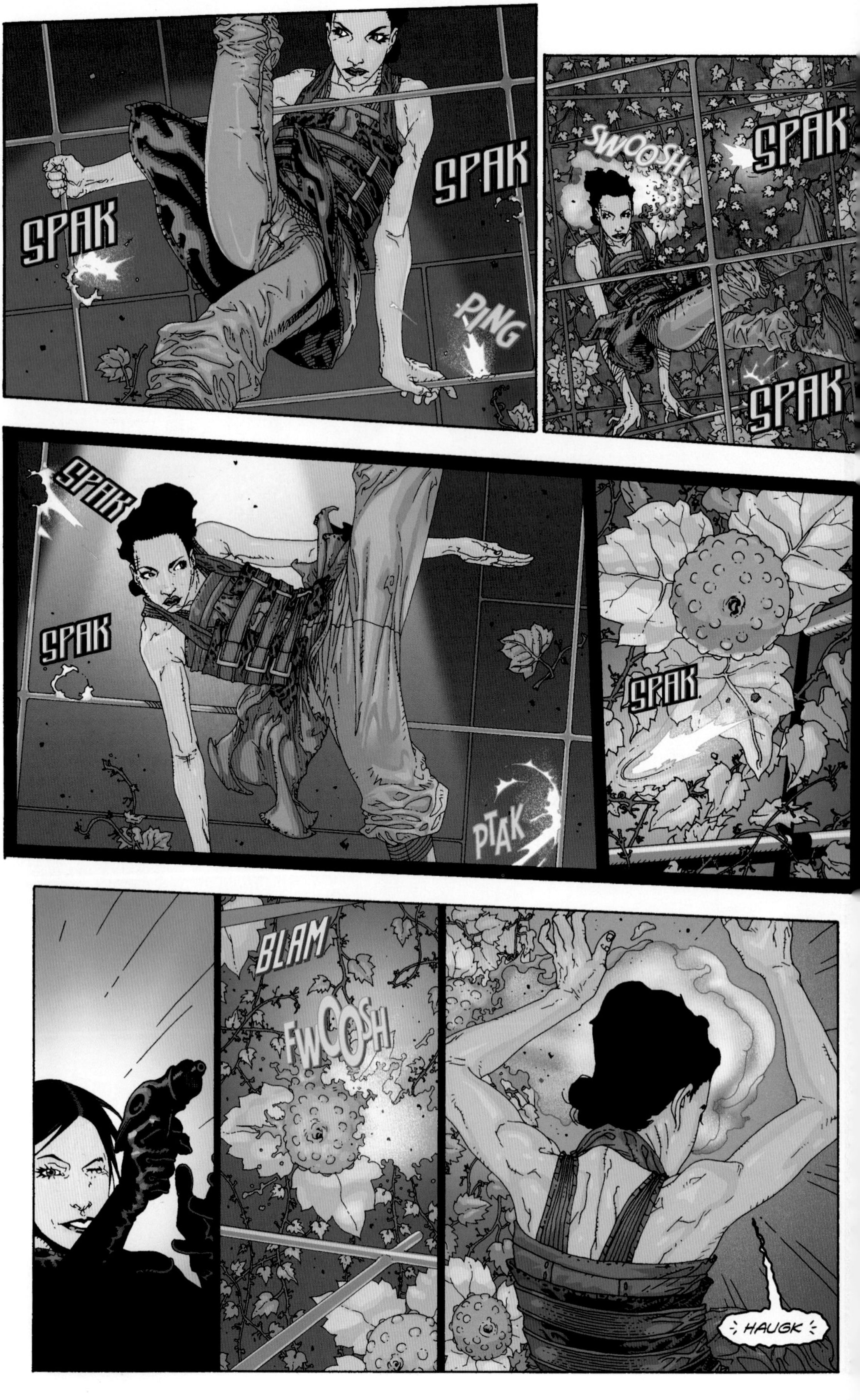
SPAK
SPAK
PING
SWOOSH
SPAK
SPAK
SPAK
SPAK
PTAK
SPAK
BLAM
FWCOOSH
HAUGK

LOOK BACK TOO OFTEN AND YOU LOSE SIGHT OF THE DANGER AHEAD.

YOU HAVE TO BE AWARE OF ALL THINGS AROUND YOU.

...WHUGK... WHEN WILL THIS "TRAINING" BE DONE...?

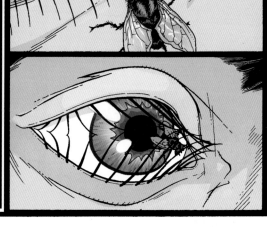

WHEN YOU CAN DO THIS.

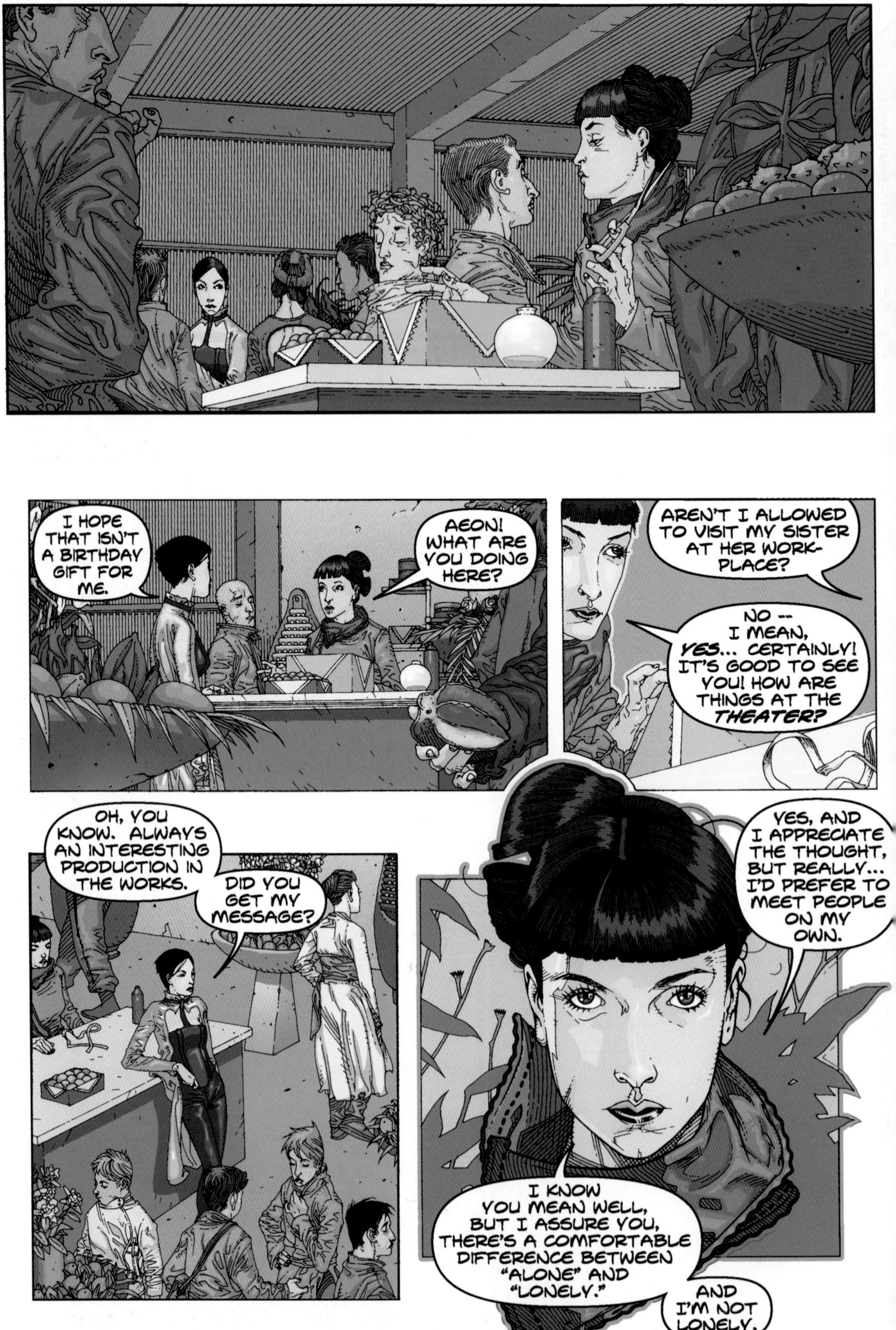
I HOPE THAT ISN'T A BIRTHDAY GIFT FOR ME.
AEON! WHAT ARE YOU DOING HERE?
AREN'T I ALLOWED TO VISIT MY SISTER AT HER WORK-PLACE?
NO -- I MEAN, *YES*... CERTAINLY! IT'S GOOD TO SEE YOU! HOW ARE THINGS AT THE *THEATER?*
OH, YOU KNOW. ALWAYS AN INTERESTING PRODUCTION IN THE WORKS.
DID YOU GET MY MESSAGE?
YES, AND I APPRECIATE THE THOUGHT, BUT REALLY... I'D PREFER TO MEET PEOPLE ON MY OWN.
I KNOW YOU MEAN WELL, BUT I ASSURE YOU, THERE'S A COMFORTABLE DIFFERENCE BETWEEN "ALONE" AND "LONELY."
AND I'M NOT LONELY.

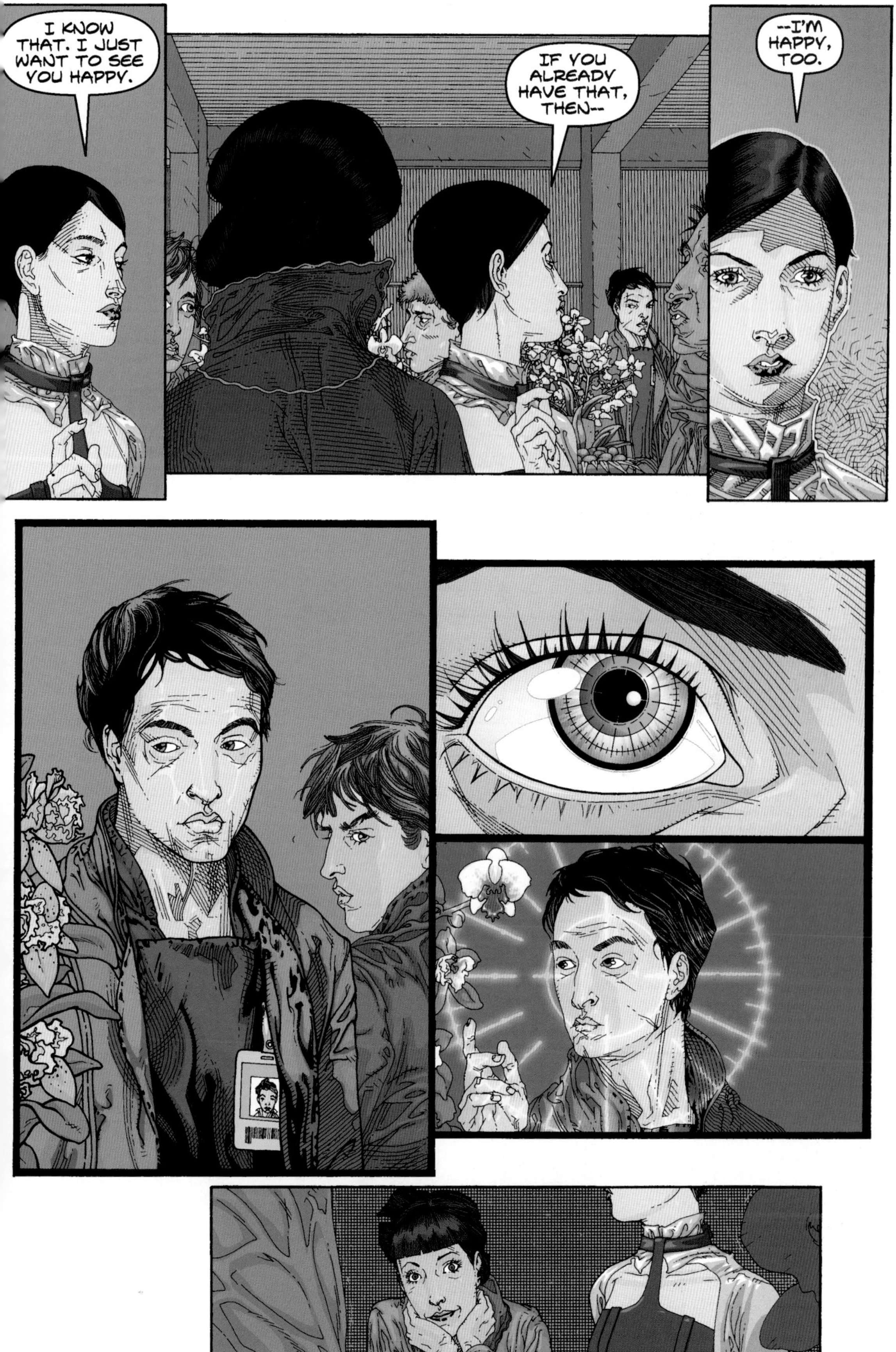
I KNOW THAT. I JUST WANT TO SEE YOU HAPPY.
IF YOU ALREADY HAVE THAT, THEN--
--I'M HAPPY, TOO.

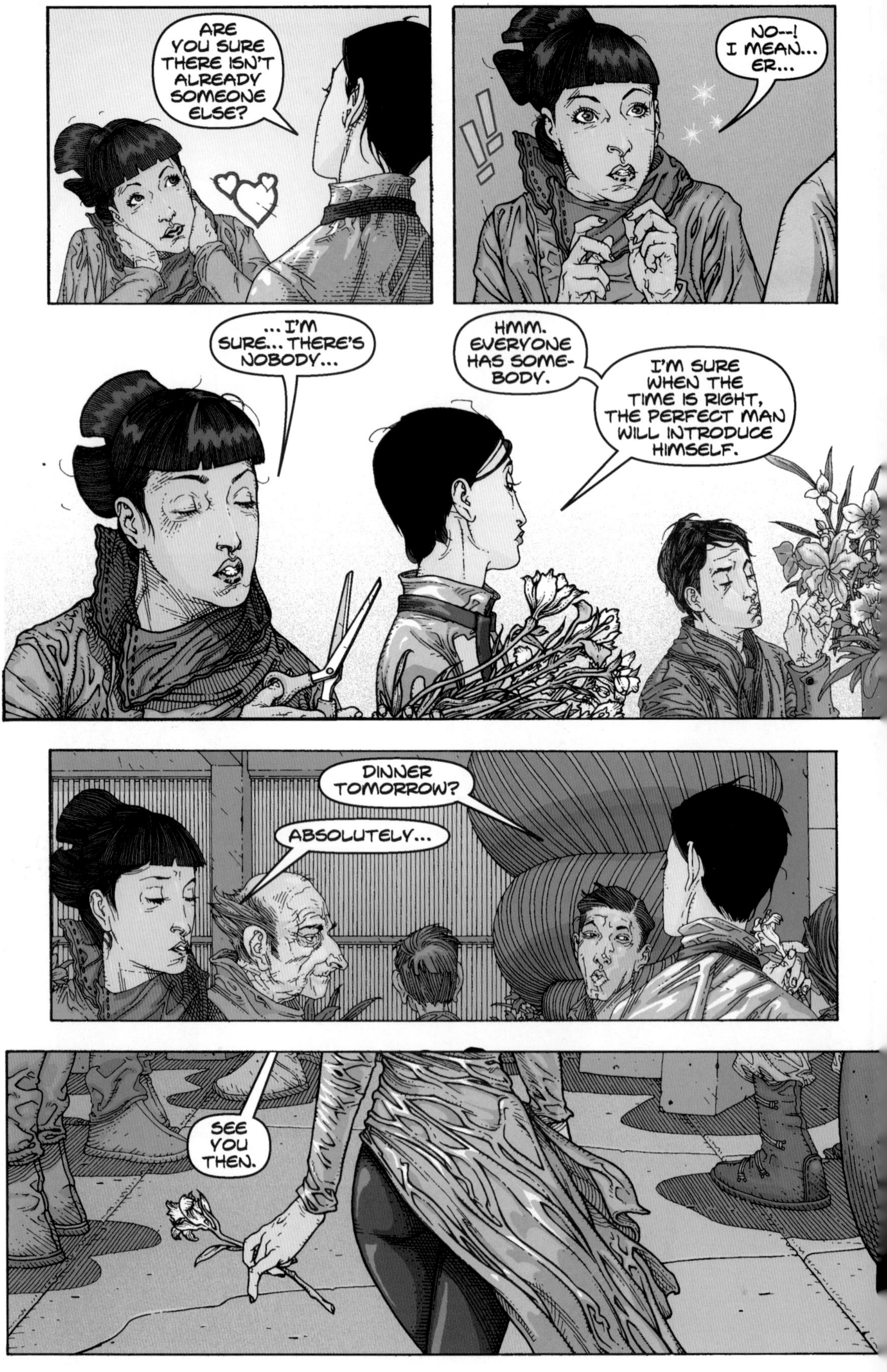
ARE YOU SURE THERE ISN'T ALREADY SOMEONE ELSE?
!!
NO--! I MEAN... ER...
...I'M SURE... THERE'S NOBODY...
HMM. EVERYONE HAS SOME-BODY.
I'M SURE WHEN THE TIME IS RIGHT, THE PERFECT MAN WILL INTRODUCE HIMSELF.
DINNER TOMORROW?
ABSOLUTELY...
SEE YOU THEN.

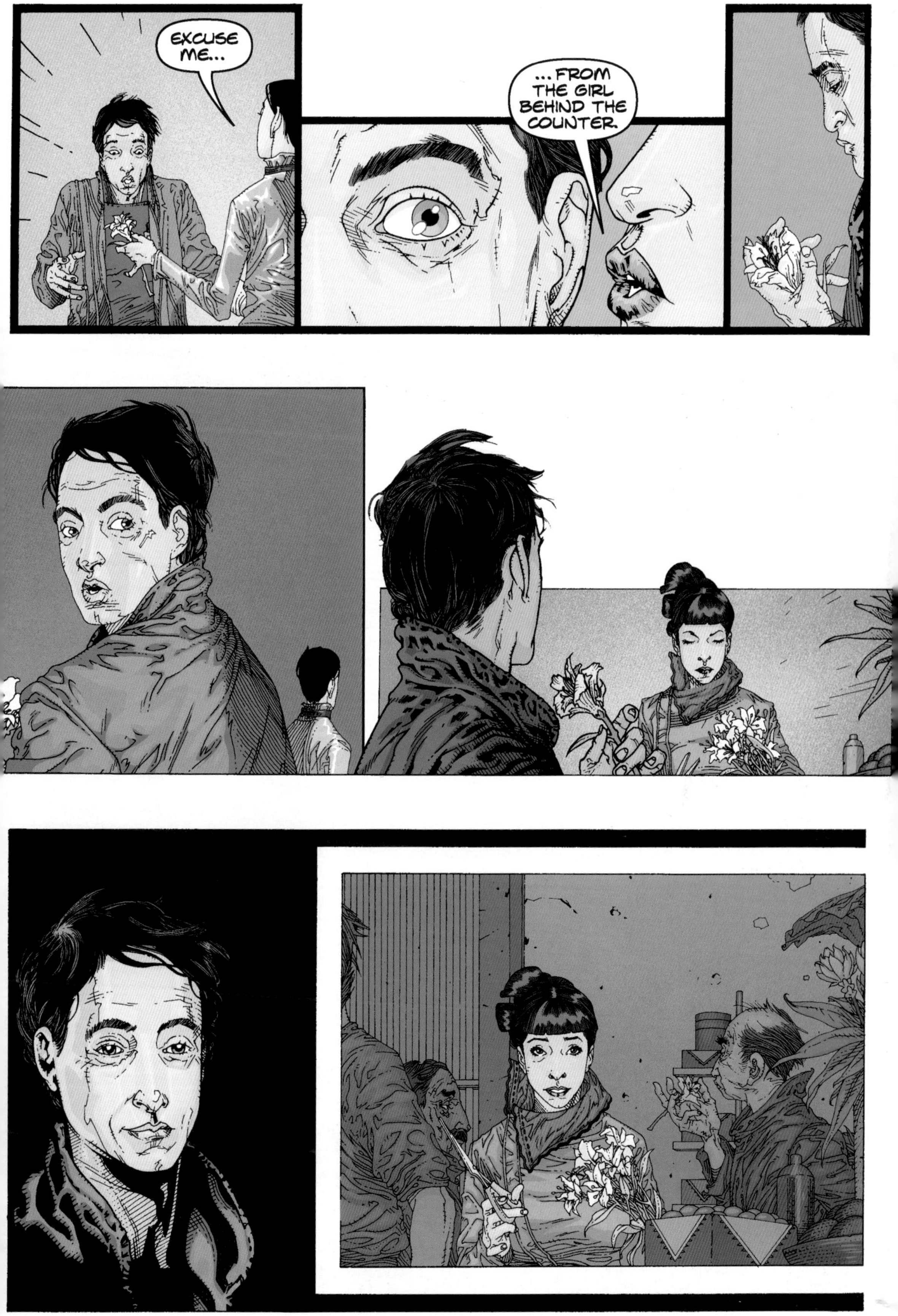
EXCUSE ME...
...FROM THE GIRL BEHIND THE COUNTER.

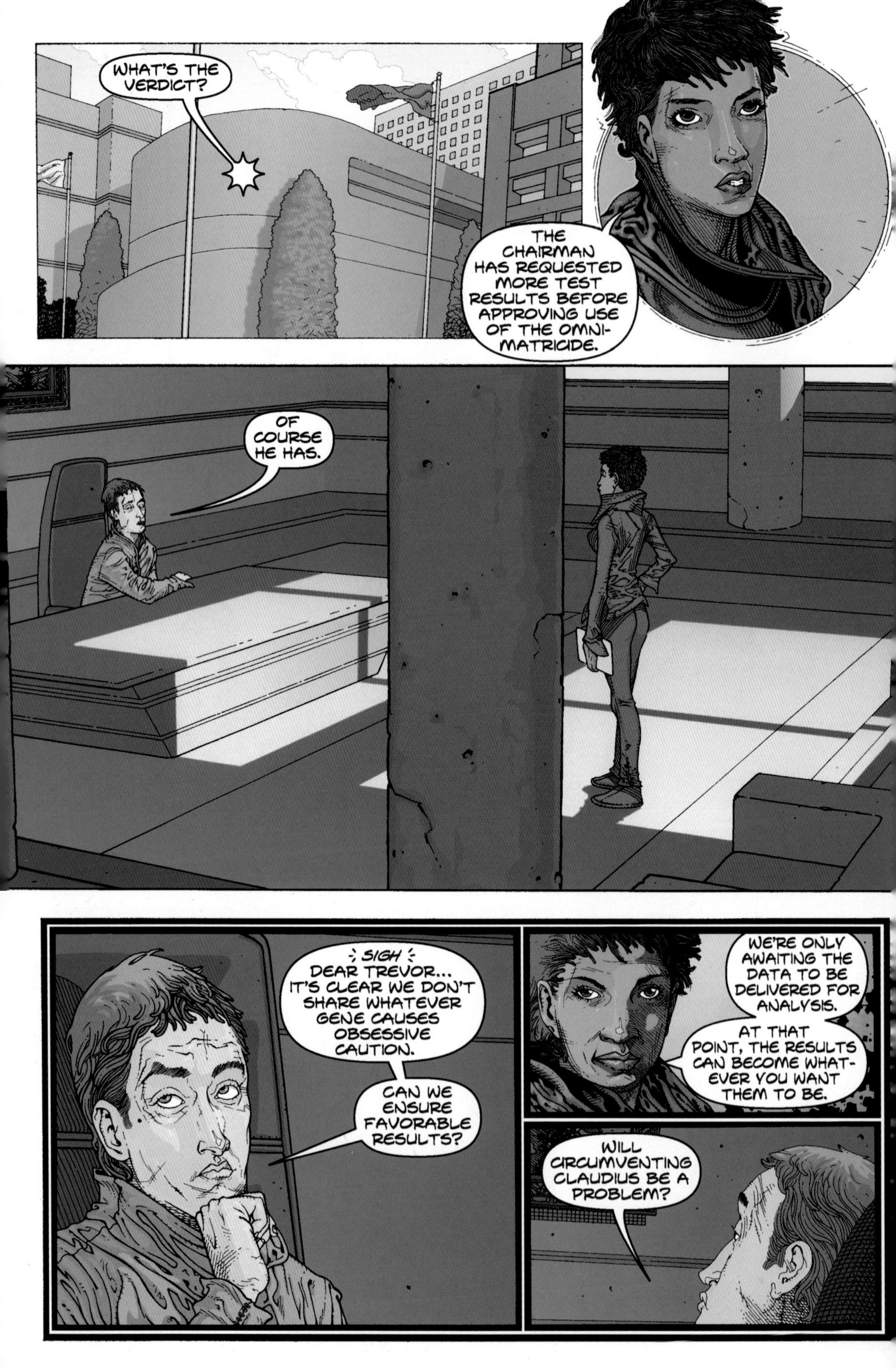
WHAT'S THE VERDICT?
THE CHAIRMAN HAS REQUESTED MORE TEST RESULTS BEFORE APPROVING USE OF THE OMNI-MATRICIDE.
OF COURSE HE HAS.
SIGH
DEAR TREVOR... IT'S CLEAR WE DON'T SHARE WHATEVER GENE CAUSES OBSESSIVE CAUTION.
CAN WE ENSURE FAVORABLE RESULTS?
WE'RE ONLY AWAITING THE DATA TO BE DELIVERED FOR ANALYSIS.
AT THAT POINT, THE RESULTS CAN BECOME WHAT-EVER YOU WANT THEM TO BE.
WILL CIRCUMVENTING CLAUDIUS BE A PROBLEM?

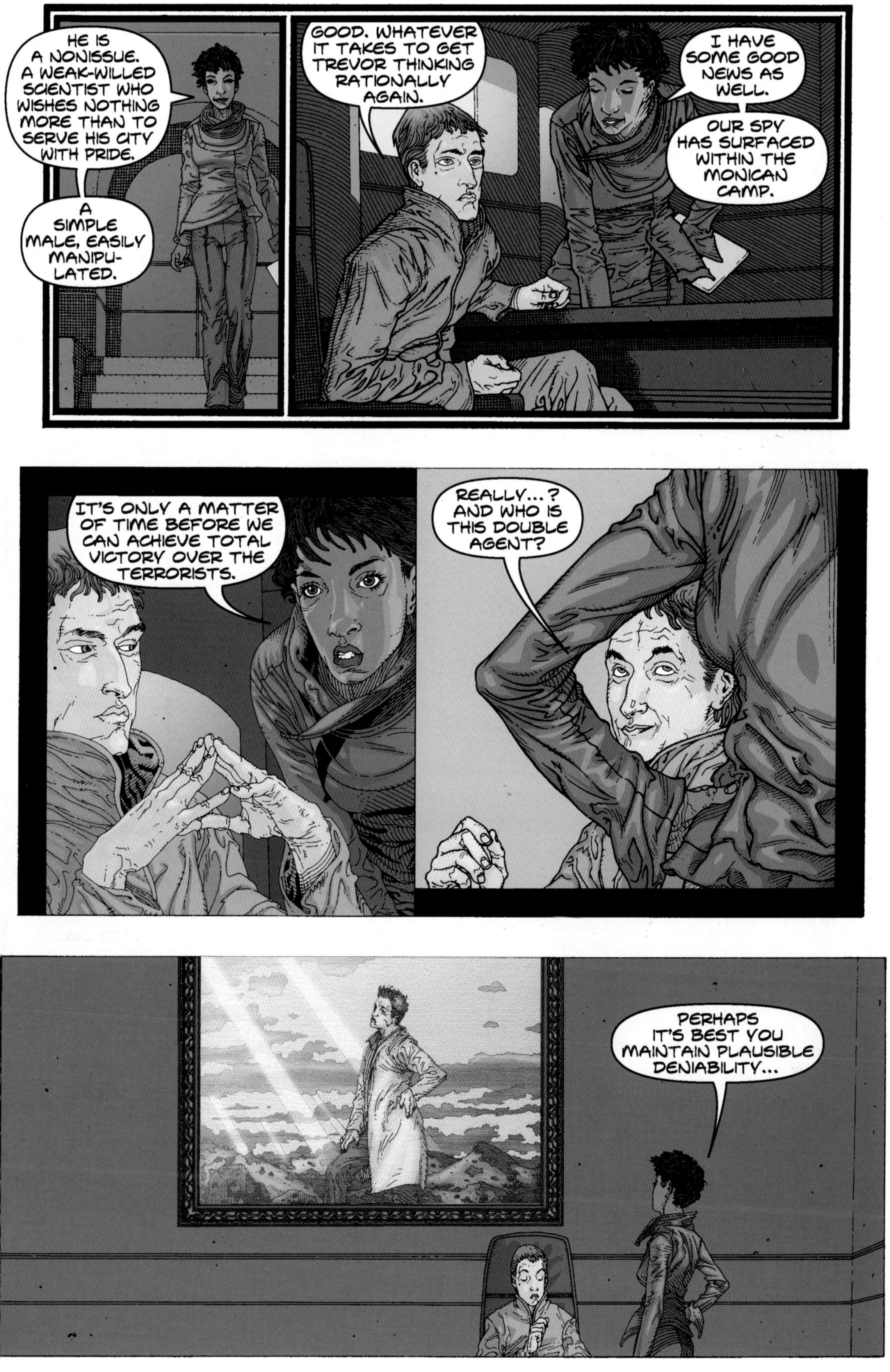
HE IS A NONISSUE. A WEAK-WILLED SCIENTIST WHO WISHES NOTHING MORE THAN TO SERVE HIS CITY WITH PRIDE.
A SIMPLE MALE, EASILY MANIPULATED.
GOOD. WHATEVER IT TAKES TO GET TREVOR THINKING RATIONALLY AGAIN.
I HAVE SOME GOOD NEWS AS WELL.
OUR SPY HAS SURFACED WITHIN THE MONICAN CAMP.
IT'S ONLY A MATTER OF TIME BEFORE WE CAN ACHIEVE TOTAL VICTORY OVER THE TERRORISTS.
REALLY...? AND WHO IS THIS DOUBLE AGENT?
PERHAPS IT'S BEST YOU MAINTAIN PLAUSIBLE DENIABILITY...

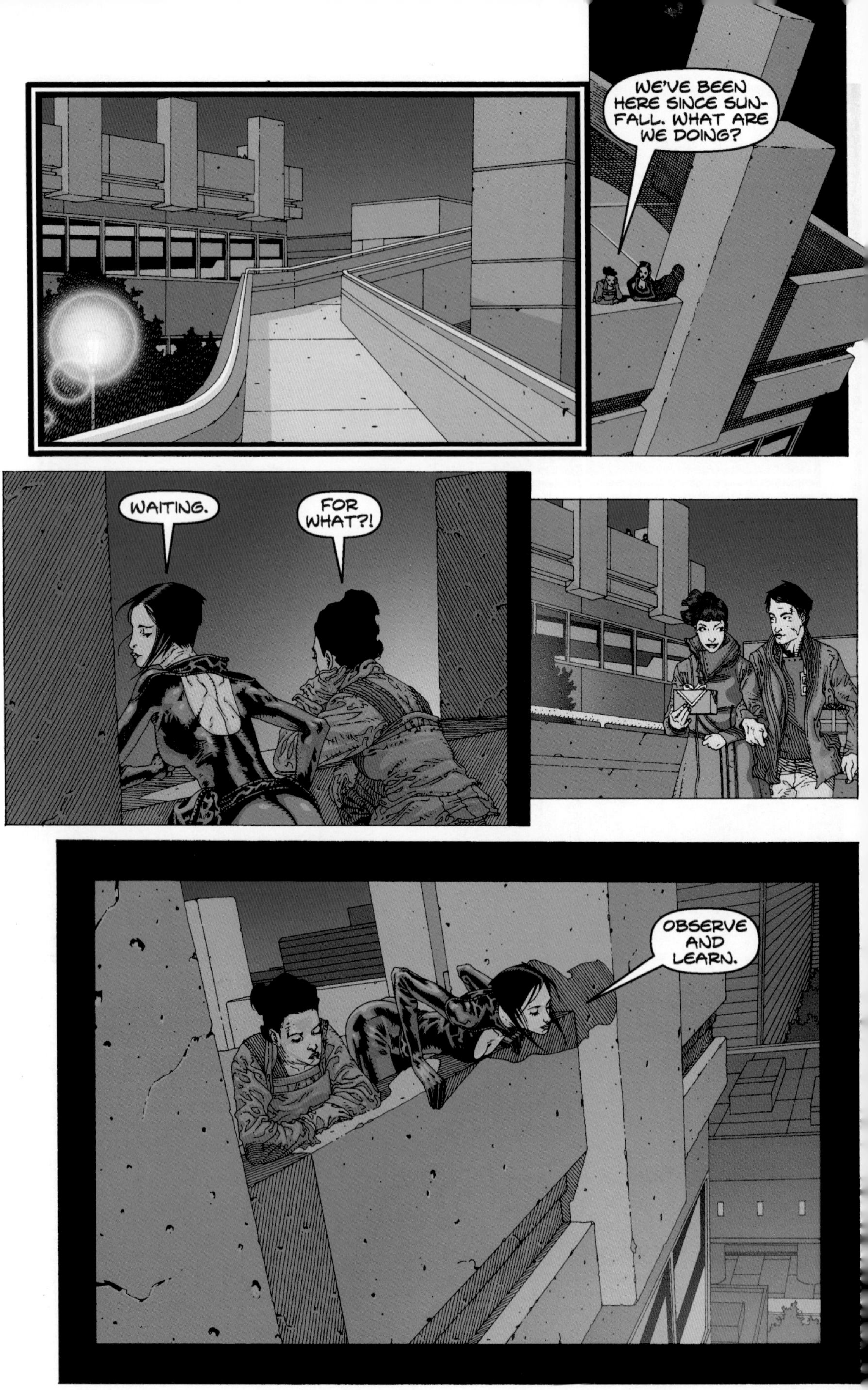
WE'VE BEEN HERE SINCE SUN-FALL. WHAT ARE WE DOING?
WAITING.
FOR WHAT?!
OBSERVE AND LEARN.

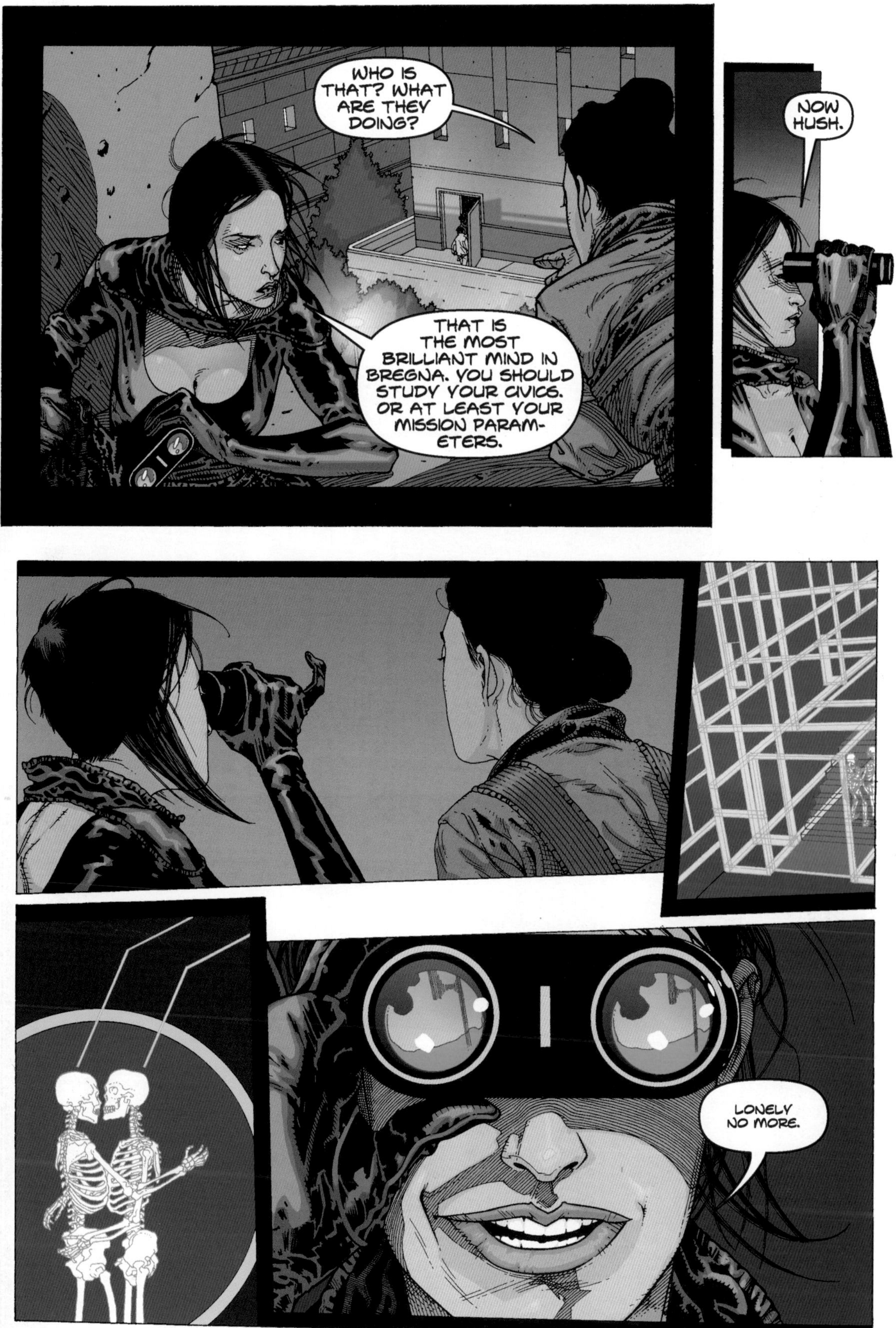
WHO IS THAT? WHAT ARE THEY DOING?
THAT IS THE MOST BRILLIANT MIND IN BREGNA. YOU SHOULD STUDY YOUR CIVICS. OR AT LEAST YOUR MISSION PARAM-ETERS.
NOW HUSH.
LONELY NO MORE.

WHERE ARE YOU GOING?
WAIT HERE.
WE'RE WASTING TIME...
HMM.

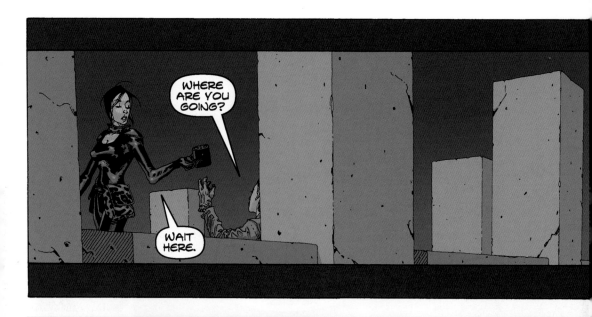

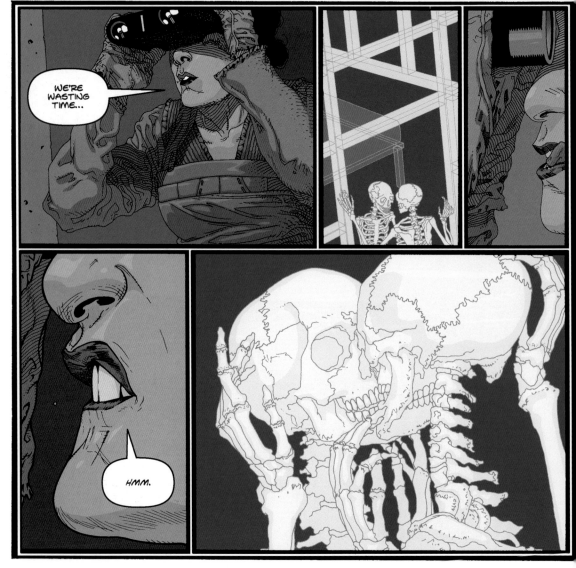

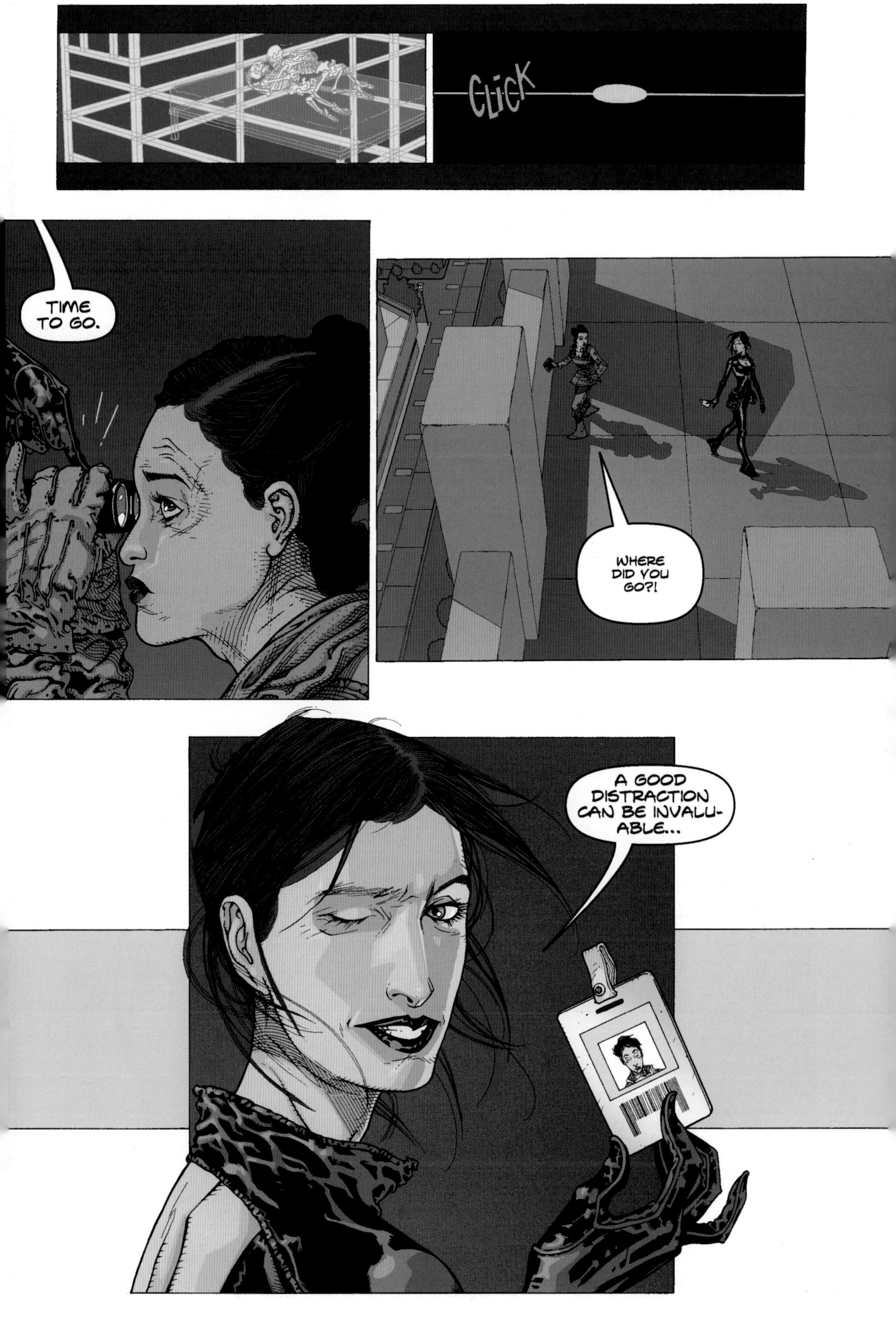
CLICK
TIME TO GO.
WHERE DID YOU GO?!
A GOOD DISTRACTION CAN BE INVALU-ABLE...

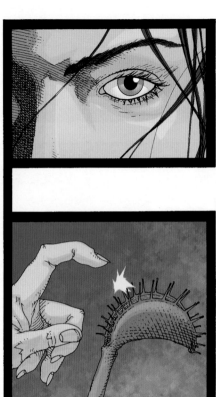

TICK.

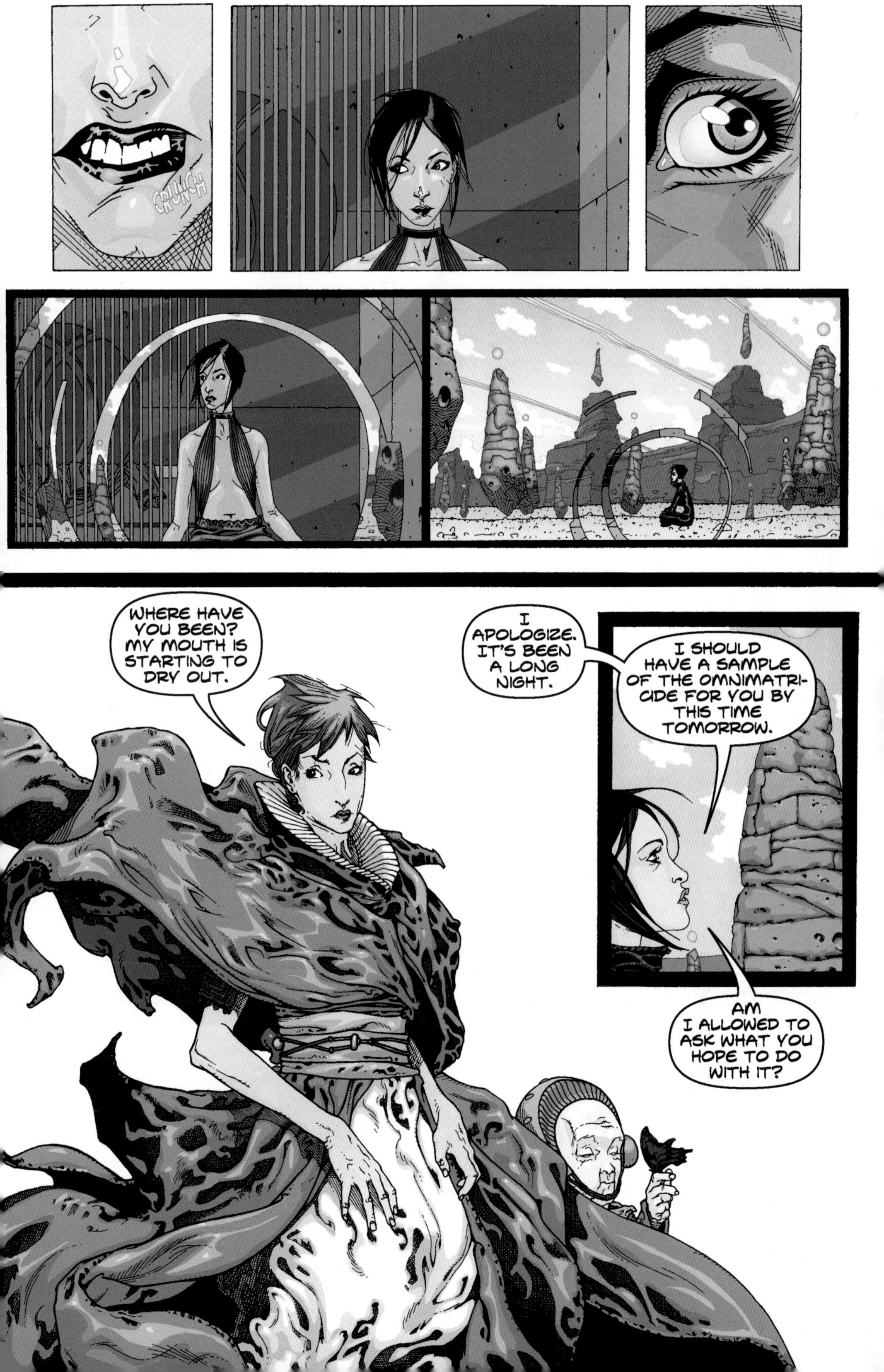
CRUNCH
WHERE HAVE YOU BEEN? MY MOUTH IS STARTING TO DRY OUT.
I APOLOGIZE. IT'S BEEN A LONG NIGHT.
I SHOULD HAVE A SAMPLE OF THE OMNIMATRI-CIDE FOR YOU BY THIS TIME TOMORROW.
AM I ALLOWED TO ASK WHAT YOU HOPE TO DO WITH IT?

I HOPE TO DEVELOP A SECOND-STAGE CHEMICAL THAT, WHEN COMBINED WITH THE OMNIMATRICIDE, WILL TURN THEIR PERFECT DEFOLIANT INTO AN INORGANIC ACID...

...THAT WILL EAT THROUGH THE CITY WALLS THEMSELVES, WEAKENING THEM ENOUGH FOR THE JUNGLE TO FINALLY PUSH THROUGH.

NOT ONLY WILL THE JUNGLE TEAR DOWN THE WALLS FOR US, BUT IT WILL DO SO WITHOUT ENDANGERING A SINGLE LIFE.

I LIKE IT -- DEVIOUS AND DESTRUCTIVE.

BUT WHY IS SITHANDRA'S PARTICIPATION SO NECESSARY?

I'VE EXPLAINED THIS ALREADY. SHE IS A USEFUL COMMODITY WHOSE ROLE WILL SERVE OUR CAUSE.

IF YOU CANNOT ACCEPT THIS TASK AS IT WAS ASSIGNED, I WOULD HAVE TO QUESTION YOUR OWN USEFULNESS.

AGAIN, I APOLOGIZE. I CERTAINLY DON'T MEAN TO QUESTION YOUR JUDGMENT.

WILL YOU EXCUSE ME A MOMENT?

BY ALL MEANS...

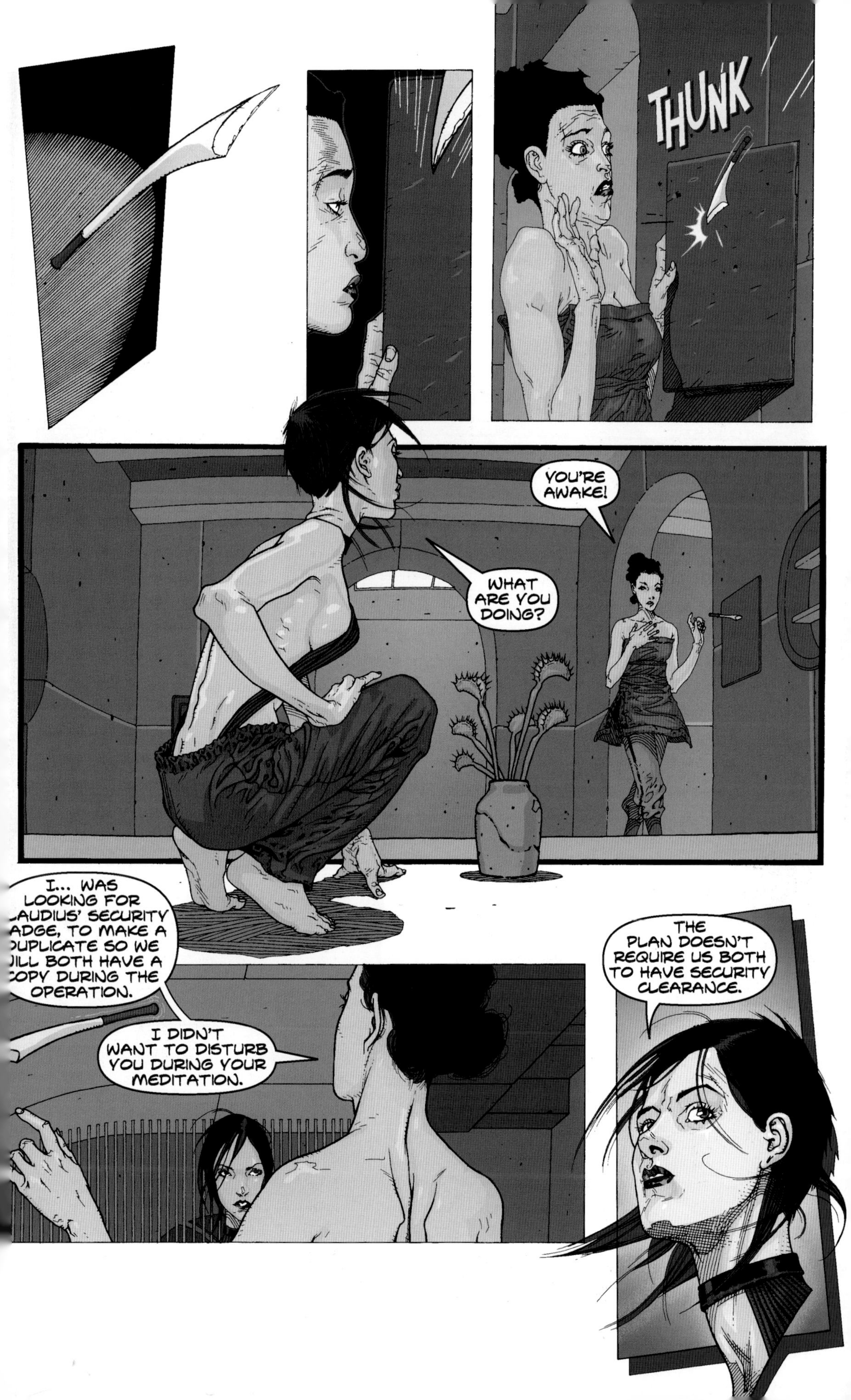
THUNK
YOU'RE AWAKE!
WHAT ARE YOU DOING?
I... WAS LOOKING FOR LAUDIUS' SECURITY ADGE, TO MAKE A UPLICATE SO WE ILL BOTH HAVE A OPY DURING THE OPERATION.
I DIDN'T WANT TO DISTURB YOU DURING YOUR MEDITATION.
THE PLAN DOESN'T REQUIRE US BOTH TO HAVE SECURITY CLEARANCE.

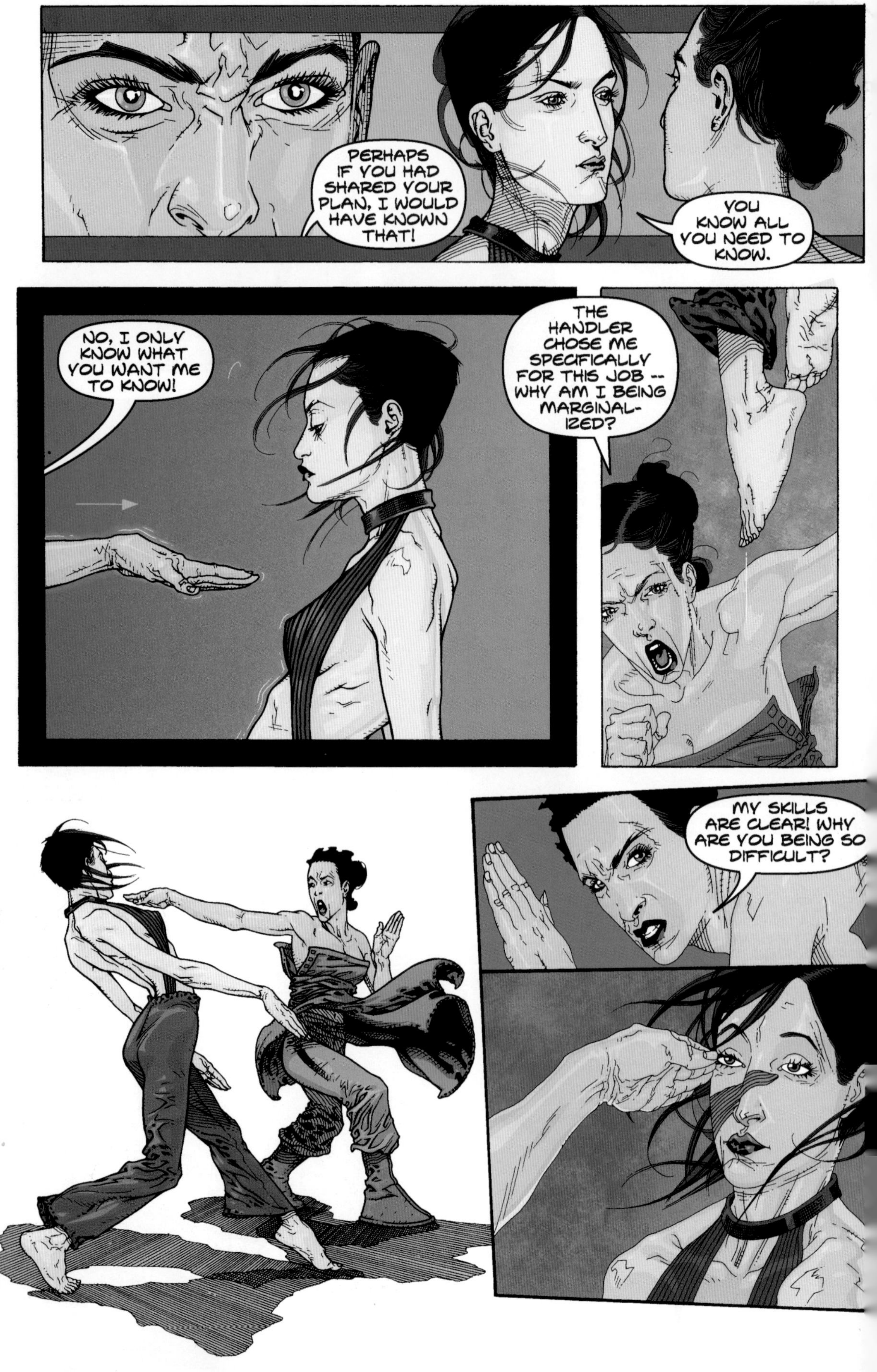
PERHAPS IF YOU HAD SHARED YOUR PLAN, I WOULD HAVE KNOWN THAT!
YOU KNOW ALL YOU NEED TO KNOW.
NO, I ONLY KNOW WHAT YOU WANT ME TO KNOW!
THE HANDLER CHOSE ME SPECIFICALLY FOR THIS JOB -- WHY AM I BEING MARGINAL-IZED?
MY SKILLS ARE CLEAR! WHY ARE YOU BEING SO DIFFICULT?

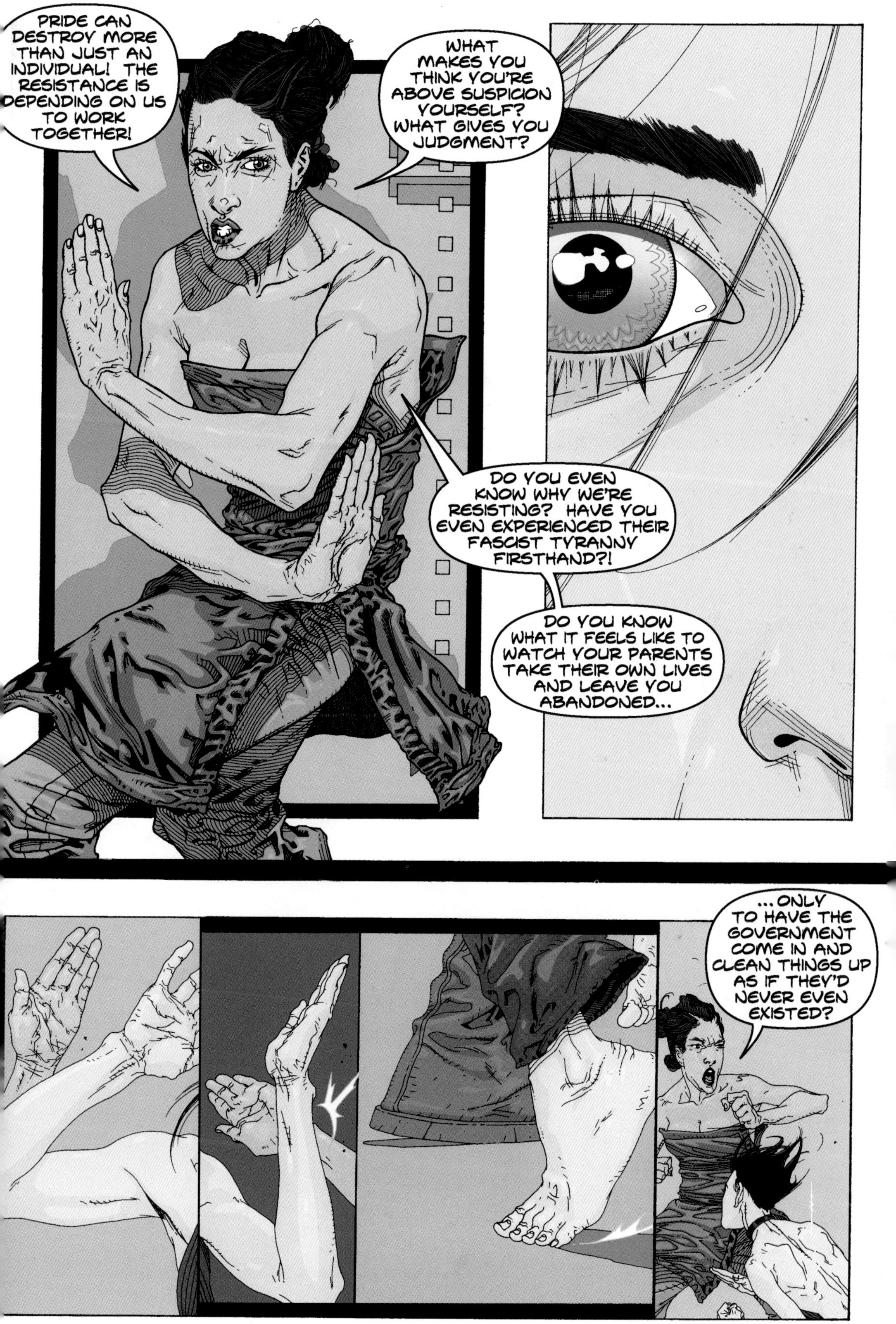
PRIDE CAN DESTROY MORE THAN JUST AN INDIVIDUAL! THE RESISTANCE IS DEPENDING ON US TO WORK TOGETHER!
WHAT MAKES YOU THINK YOU'RE ABOVE SUSPICION YOURSELF? WHAT GIVES YOU JUDGMENT?
DO YOU EVEN KNOW WHY WE'RE RESISTING? HAVE YOU EVEN EXPERIENCED THEIR FASCIST TYRANNY FIRSTHAND?!
DO YOU KNOW WHAT IT FEELS LIKE TO WATCH YOUR PARENTS TAKE THEIR OWN LIVES AND LEAVE YOU ABANDONED...
...ONLY TO HAVE THE GOVERNMENT COME IN AND CLEAN THINGS UP AS IF THEY'D NEVER EVEN EXISTED?

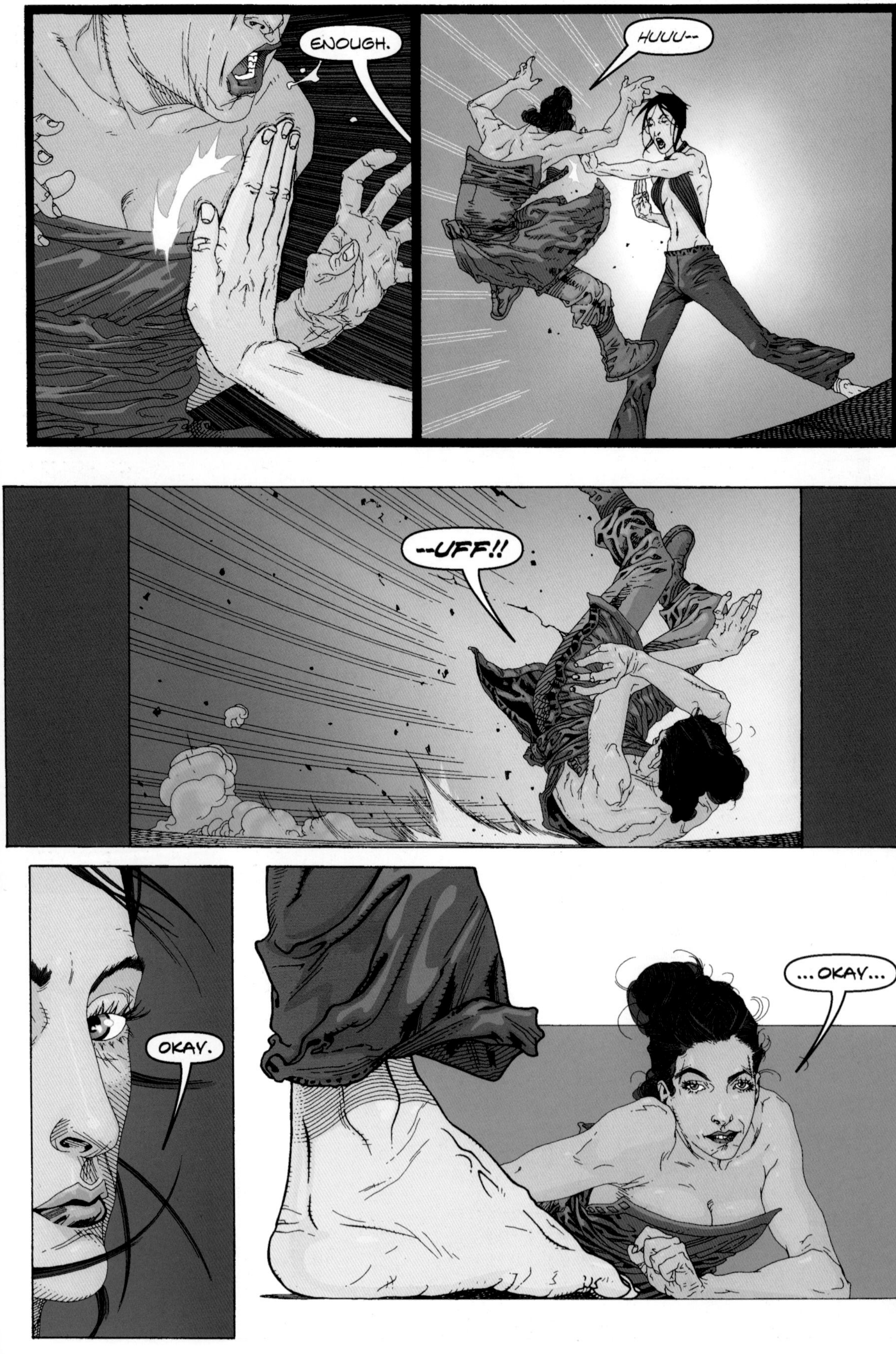
ENOUGH.
HUUU--
--UFF!!
OKAY.
...OKAY...

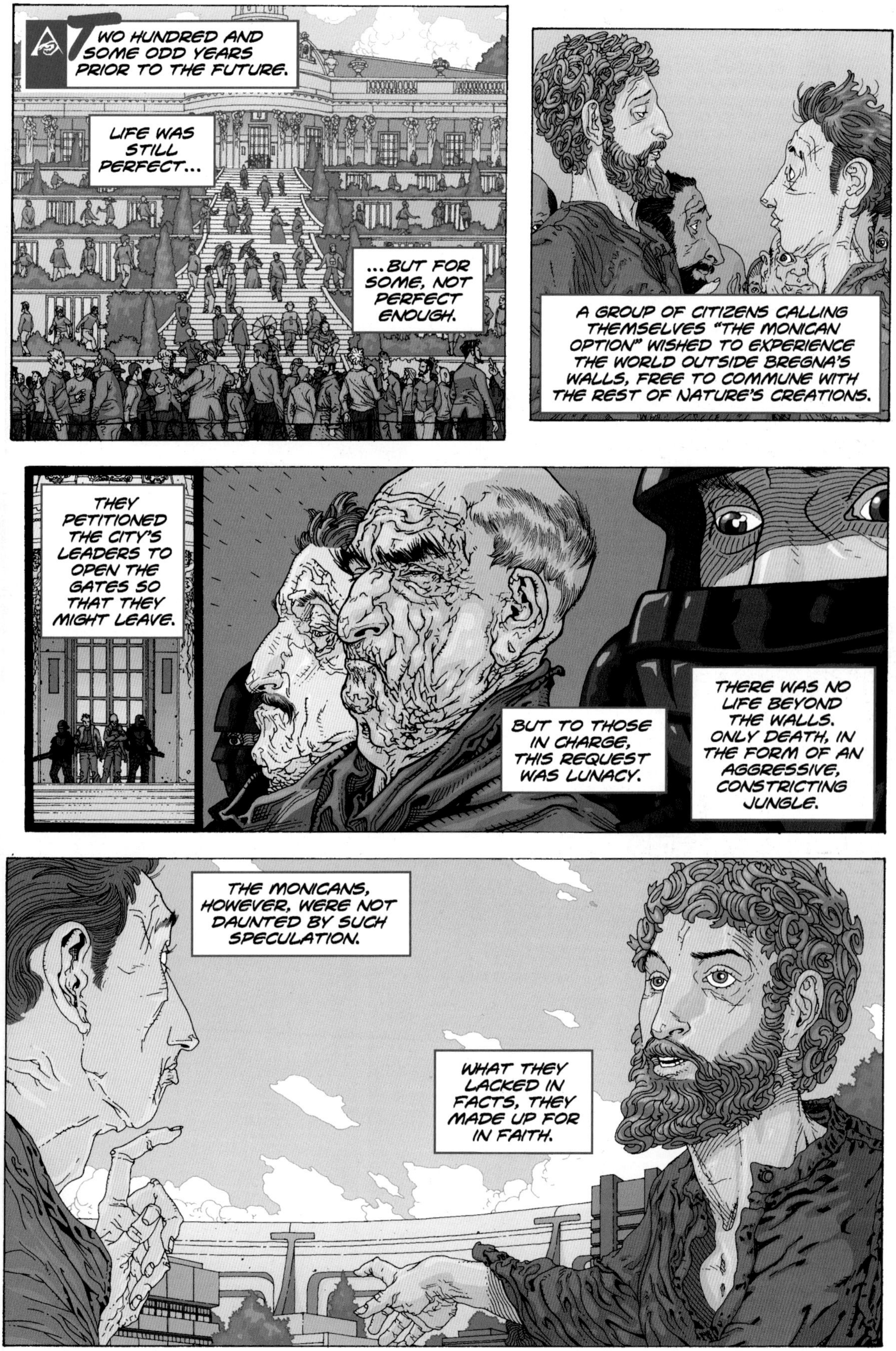
TWO HUNDRED AND SOME ODD YEARS PRIOR TO THE FUTURE.
LIFE WAS STILL PERFECT...
...BUT FOR SOME, NOT PERFECT ENOUGH.
A GROUP OF CITIZENS CALLING THEMSELVES "THE MONICAN OPTION" WISHED TO EXPERIENCE THE WORLD OUTSIDE BREGNA'S WALLS, FREE TO COMMUNE WITH THE REST OF NATURE'S CREATIONS.
THEY PETITIONED THE CITY'S LEADERS TO OPEN THE GATES SO THAT THEY MIGHT LEAVE.
BUT TO THOSE IN CHARGE, THIS REQUEST WAS LUNACY.
THERE WAS NO LIFE BEYOND THE WALLS. ONLY DEATH, IN THE FORM OF AN AGGRESSIVE, CONSTRICTING JUNGLE.
THE MONICANS, HOWEVER, WERE NOT DAUNTED BY SUCH SPECULATION.
WHAT THEY LACKED IN FACTS, THEY MADE UP FOR IN FAITH.

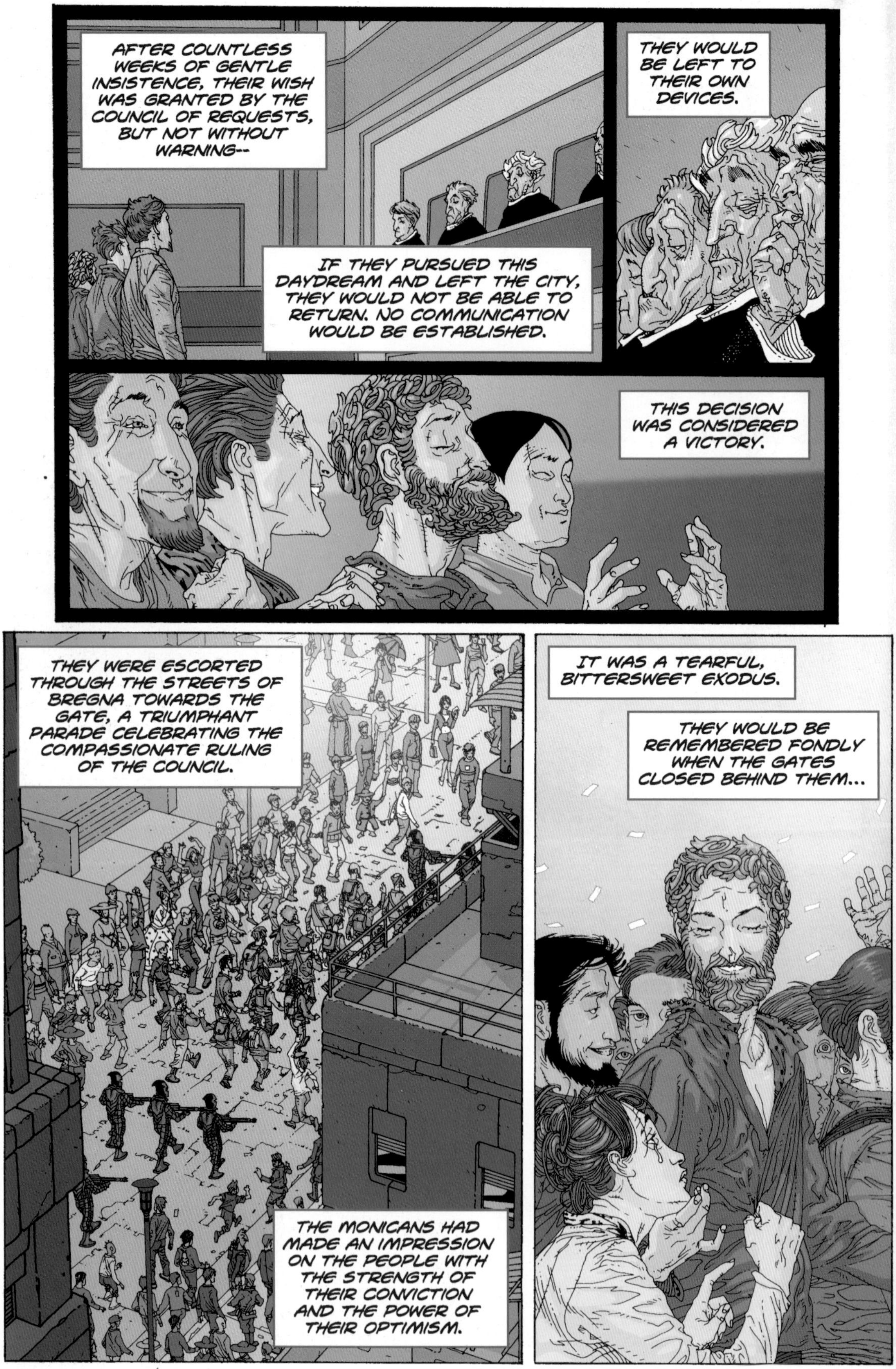
AFTER COUNTLESS WEEKS OF GENTLE INSISTENCE, THEIR WISH WAS GRANTED BY THE COUNCIL OF REQUESTS, BUT NOT WITHOUT WARNING--
IF THEY PURSUED THIS DAYDREAM AND LEFT THE CITY, THEY WOULD NOT BE ABLE TO RETURN. NO COMMUNICATION WOULD BE ESTABLISHED.
THEY WOULD BE LEFT TO THEIR OWN DEVICES.
THIS DECISION WAS CONSIDERED A VICTORY.
THEY WERE ESCORTED THROUGH THE STREETS OF BREGNA TOWARDS THE GATE, A TRIUMPHANT PARADE CELEBRATING THE COMPASSIONATE RULING OF THE COUNCIL.
THE MONICANS HAD MADE AN IMPRESSION ON THE PEOPLE WITH THE STRENGTH OF THEIR CONVICTION AND THE POWER OF THEIR OPTIMISM.
IT WAS A TEARFUL, BITTERSWEET EXODUS.
THEY WOULD BE REMEMBERED FONDLY WHEN THE GATES CLOSED BEHIND THEM...

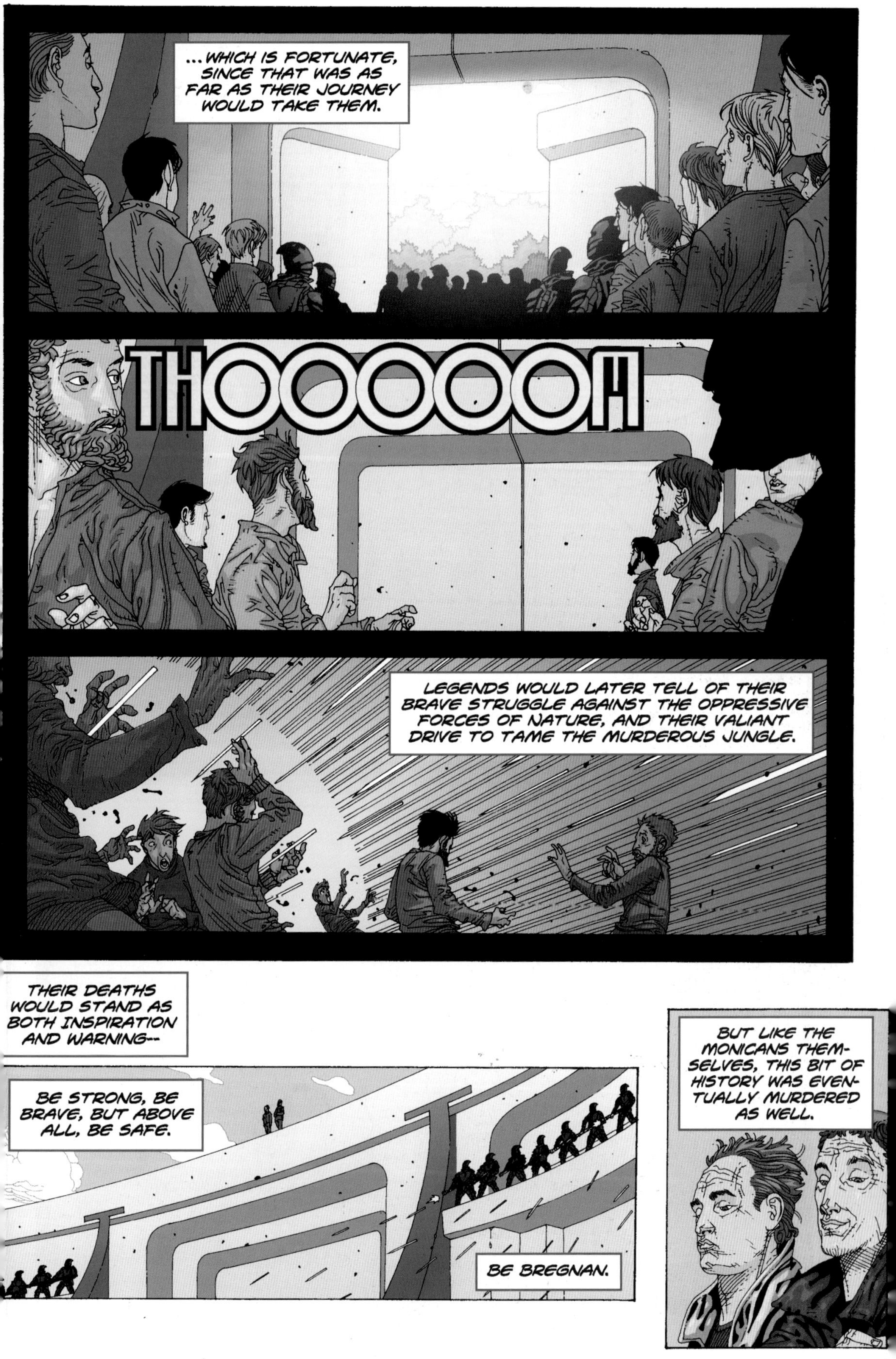
...WHICH IS FORTUNATE, SINCE THAT WAS AS FAR AS THEIR JOURNEY WOULD TAKE THEM.
THOOOOOM
LEGENDS WOULD LATER TELL OF THEIR BRAVE STRUGGLE AGAINST THE OPPRESSIVE FORCES OF NATURE, AND THEIR VALIANT DRIVE TO TAME THE MURDEROUS JUNGLE.
THEIR DEATHS WOULD STAND AS BOTH INSPIRATION AND WARNING--
BE STRONG, BE BRAVE, BUT ABOVE ALL, BE SAFE.
BE BREGNAN.
BUT LIKE THE MONICANS THEM-SELVES, THIS BIT OF HISTORY WAS EVEN-TUALLY MURDERED AS WELL.

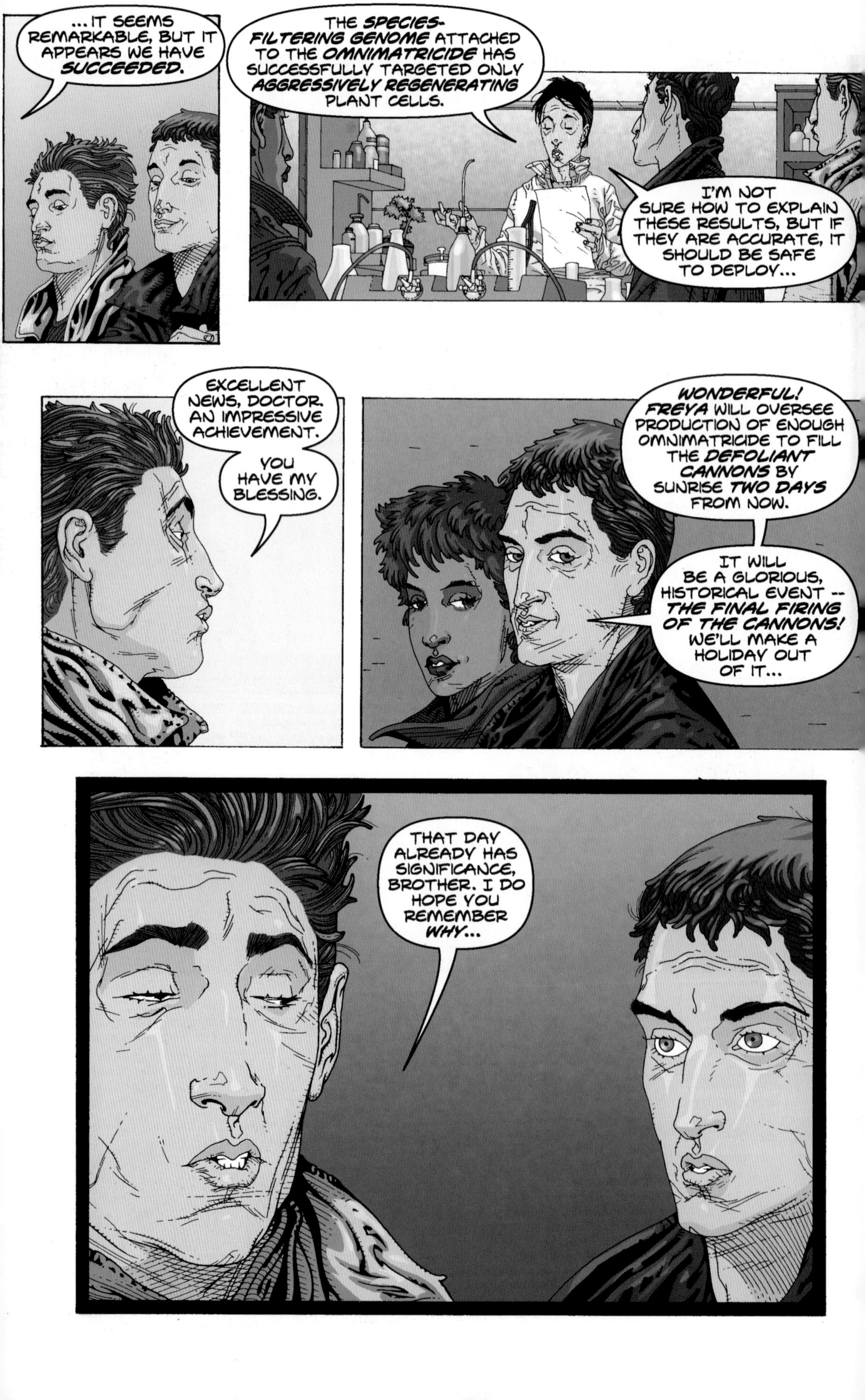
...IT SEEMS REMARKABLE, BUT IT APPEARS WE HAVE SUCCEEDED.
THE SPECIES-FILTERING GENOME ATTACHED TO THE OMNIMATRICIDE HAS SUCCESSFULLY TARGETED ONLY AGGRESSIVELY REGENERATING PLANT CELLS.
I'M NOT SURE HOW TO EXPLAIN THESE RESULTS, BUT IF THEY ARE ACCURATE, IT SHOULD BE SAFE TO DEPLOY...
EXCELLENT NEWS, DOCTOR. AN IMPRESSIVE ACHIEVEMENT.
YOU HAVE MY BLESSING.
WONDERFUL! FREYA WILL OVERSEE PRODUCTION OF ENOUGH OMNIMATRICIDE TO FILL THE DEFOLIANT CANNONS BY SUNRISE TWO DAYS FROM NOW.
IT WILL BE A GLORIOUS, HISTORICAL EVENT -- THE FINAL FIRING OF THE CANNONS! WE'LL MAKE A HOLIDAY OUT OF IT...
THAT DAY ALREADY HAS SIGNIFICANCE, BROTHER. I DO HOPE YOU REMEMBER WHY...

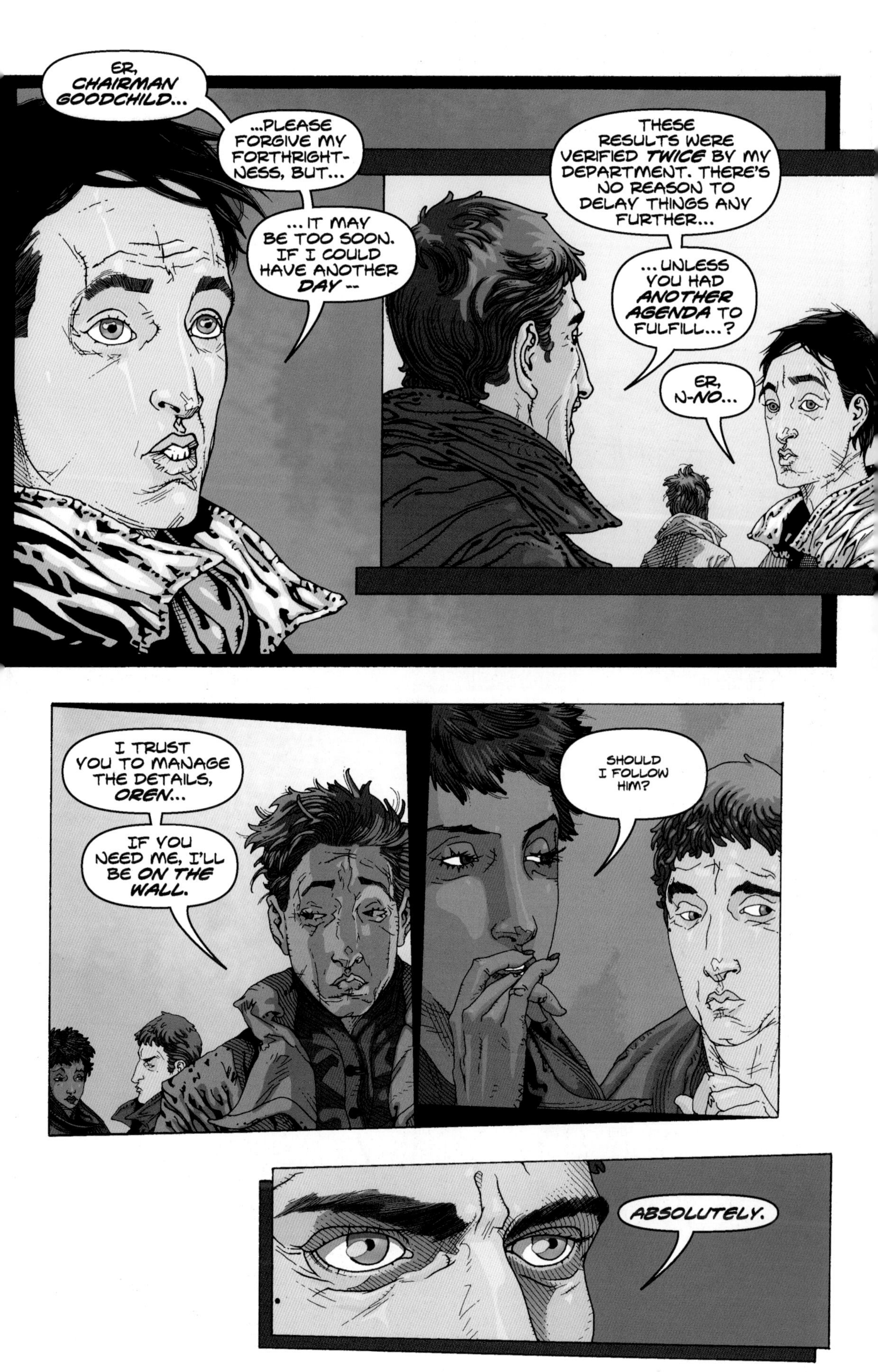
ER, CHAIRMAN GOODCHILD...
...PLEASE FORGIVE MY FORTHRIGHT-NESS, BUT...
...IT MAY BE TOO SOON. IF I COULD HAVE ANOTHER DAY --
THESE RESULTS WERE VERIFIED TWICE BY MY DEPARTMENT. THERE'S NO REASON TO DELAY THINGS ANY FURTHER...
...UNLESS YOU HAD ANOTHER AGENDA TO FULFILL...?
ER, N-NO...
I TRUST YOU TO MANAGE THE DETAILS, OREN...
IF YOU NEED ME, I'LL BE ON THE WALL.
SHOULD I FOLLOW HIM?
ABSOLUTELY.

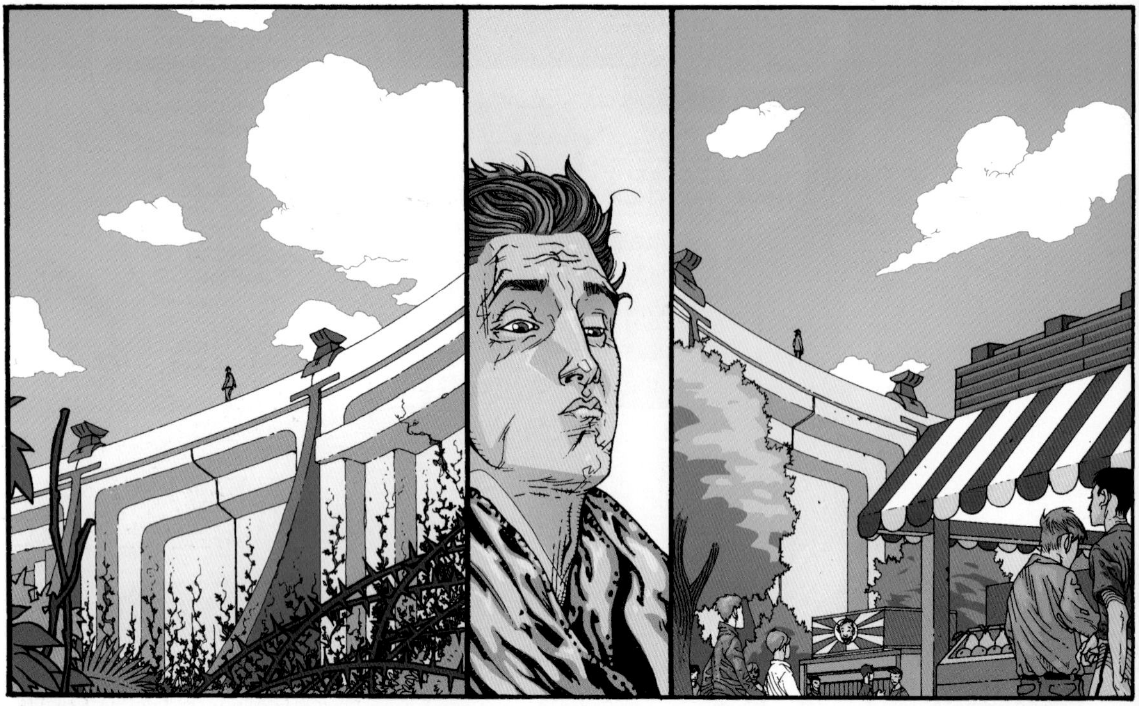

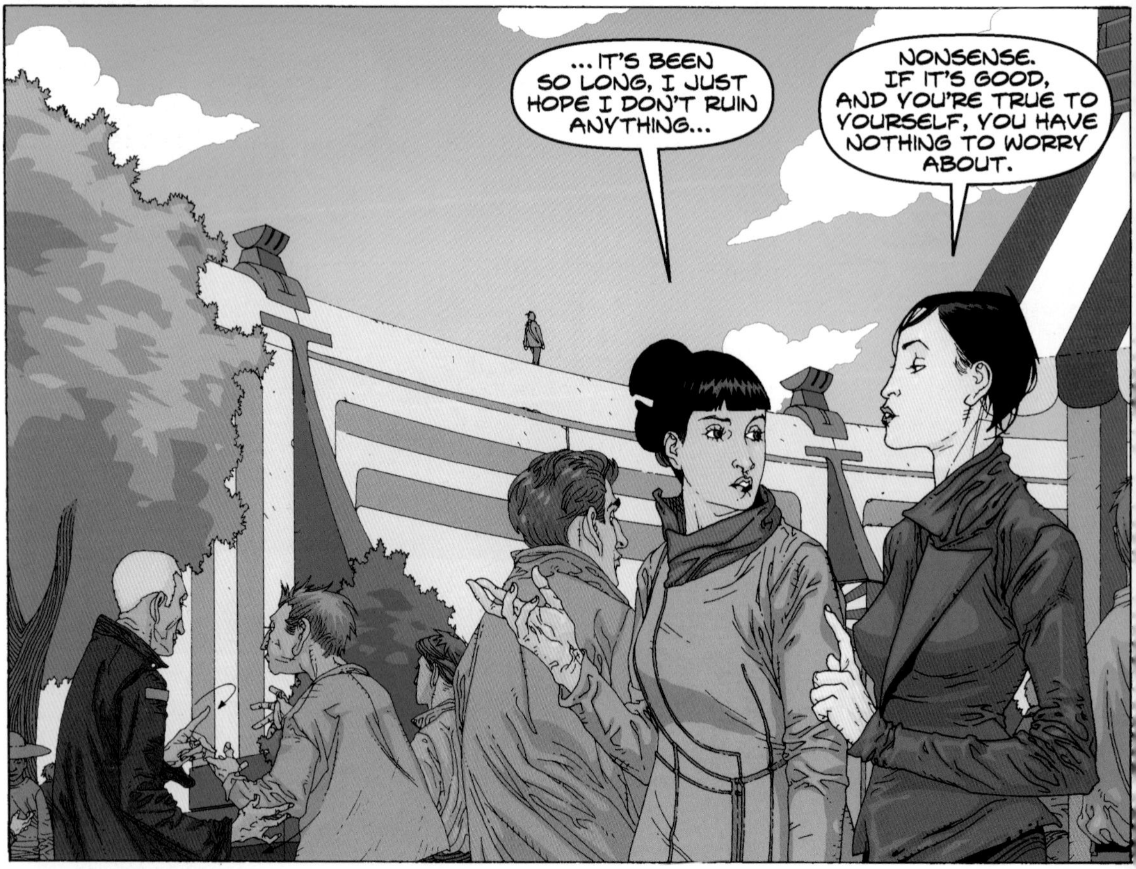
...IT'S BEEN SO LONG, I JUST HOPE I DON'T RUIN ANYTHING...
NONSENSE. IF IT'S GOOD, AND YOU'RE TRUE TO YOURSELF, YOU HAVE NOTHING TO WORRY ABOUT.

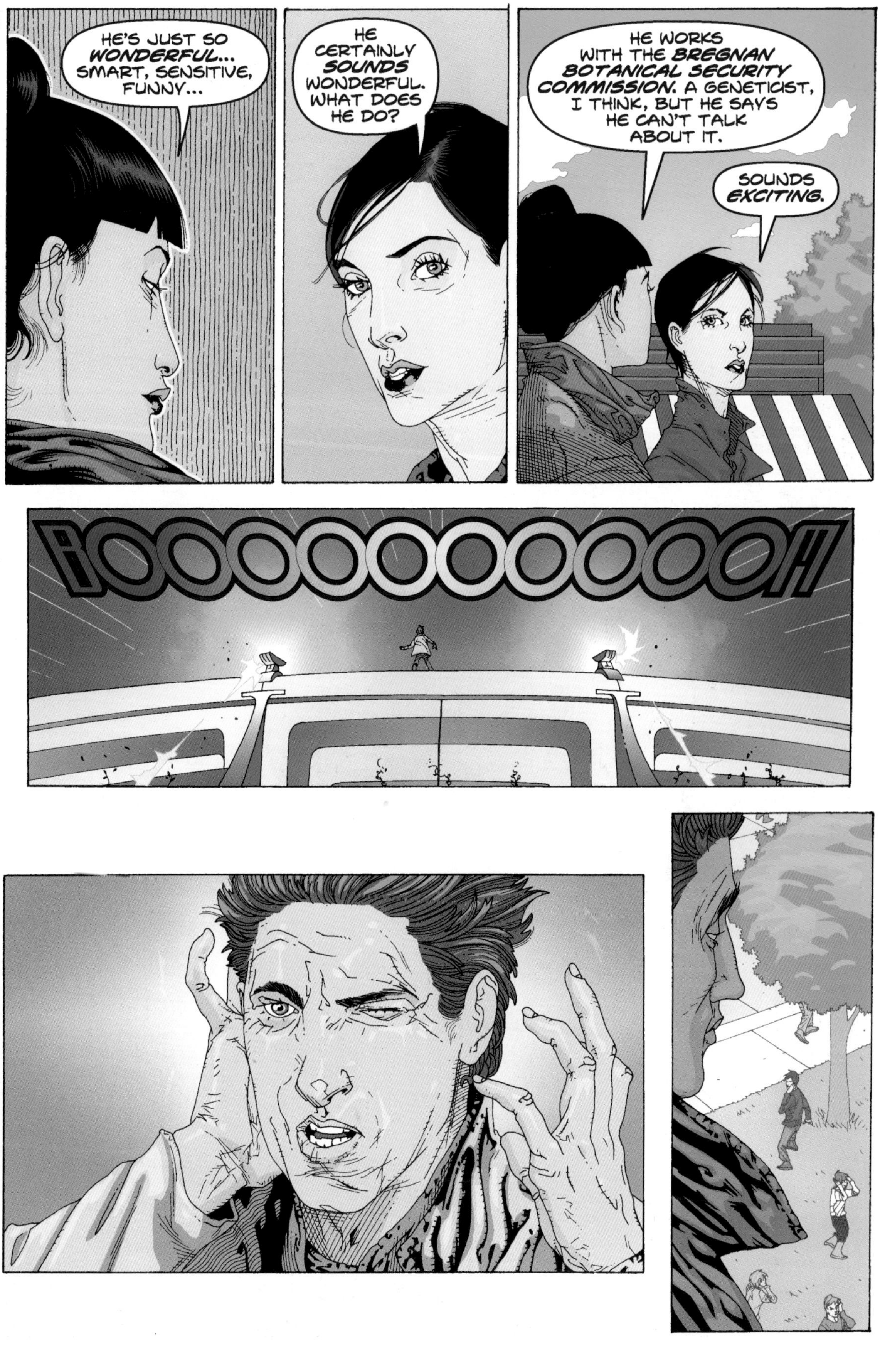
HE'S JUST SO WONDERFUL... SMART, SENSITIVE, FUNNY...
HE CERTAINLY SOUNDS WONDERFUL. WHAT DOES HE DO?
HE WORKS WITH THE BREGNAN BOTANICAL SECURITY COMMISSION. A GENETICIST, I THINK, BUT HE SAYS HE CAN'T TALK ABOUT IT.
SOUNDS EXCITING.
BOOOOOOOOOOOH

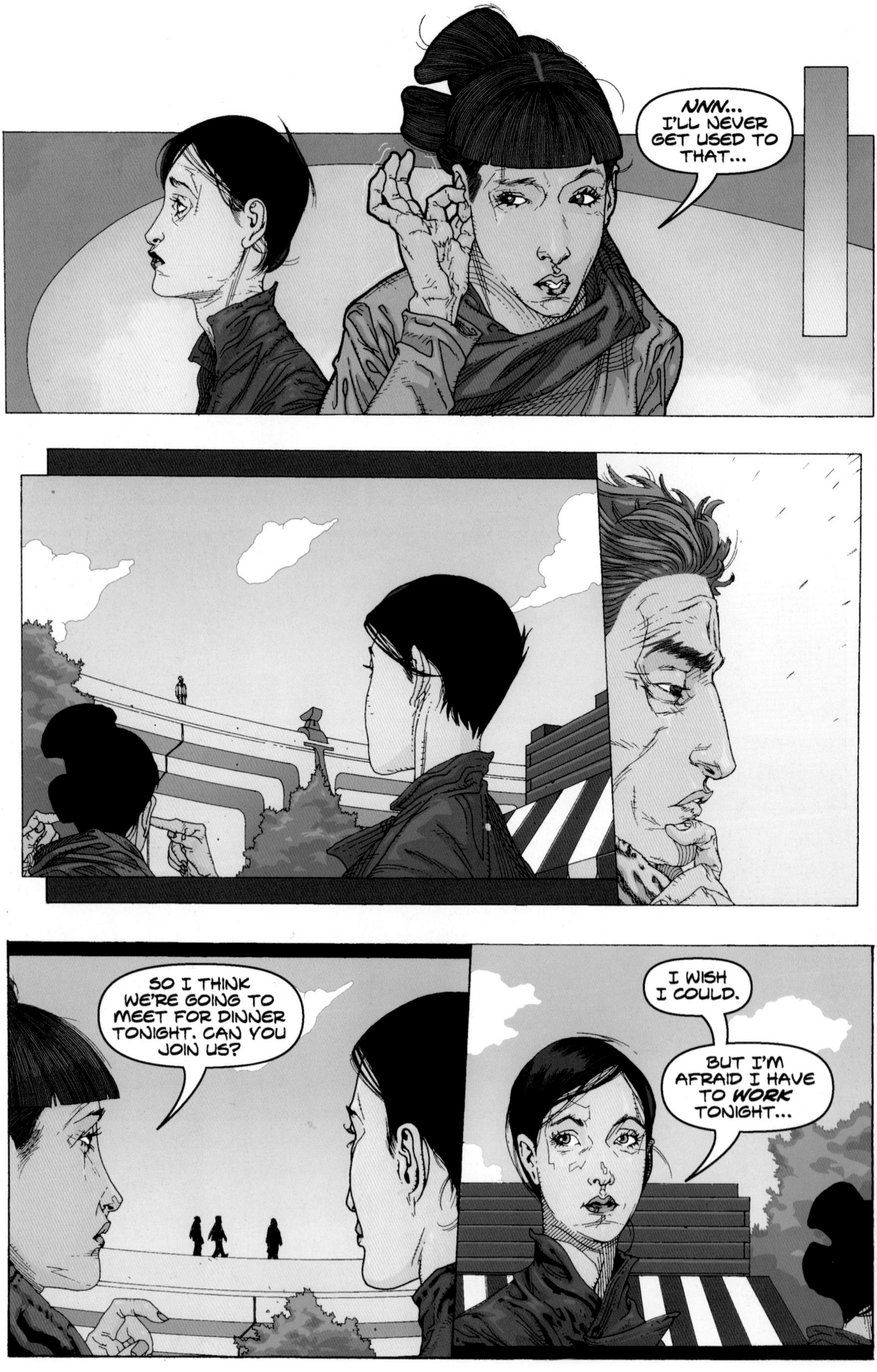
NNN... I'LL NEVER GET USED TO THAT...
SO I THINK WE'RE GOING TO MEET FOR DINNER TONIGHT. CAN YOU JOIN US?
I WISH I COULD.
BUT I'M AFRAID I HAVE TO WORK TONIGHT...

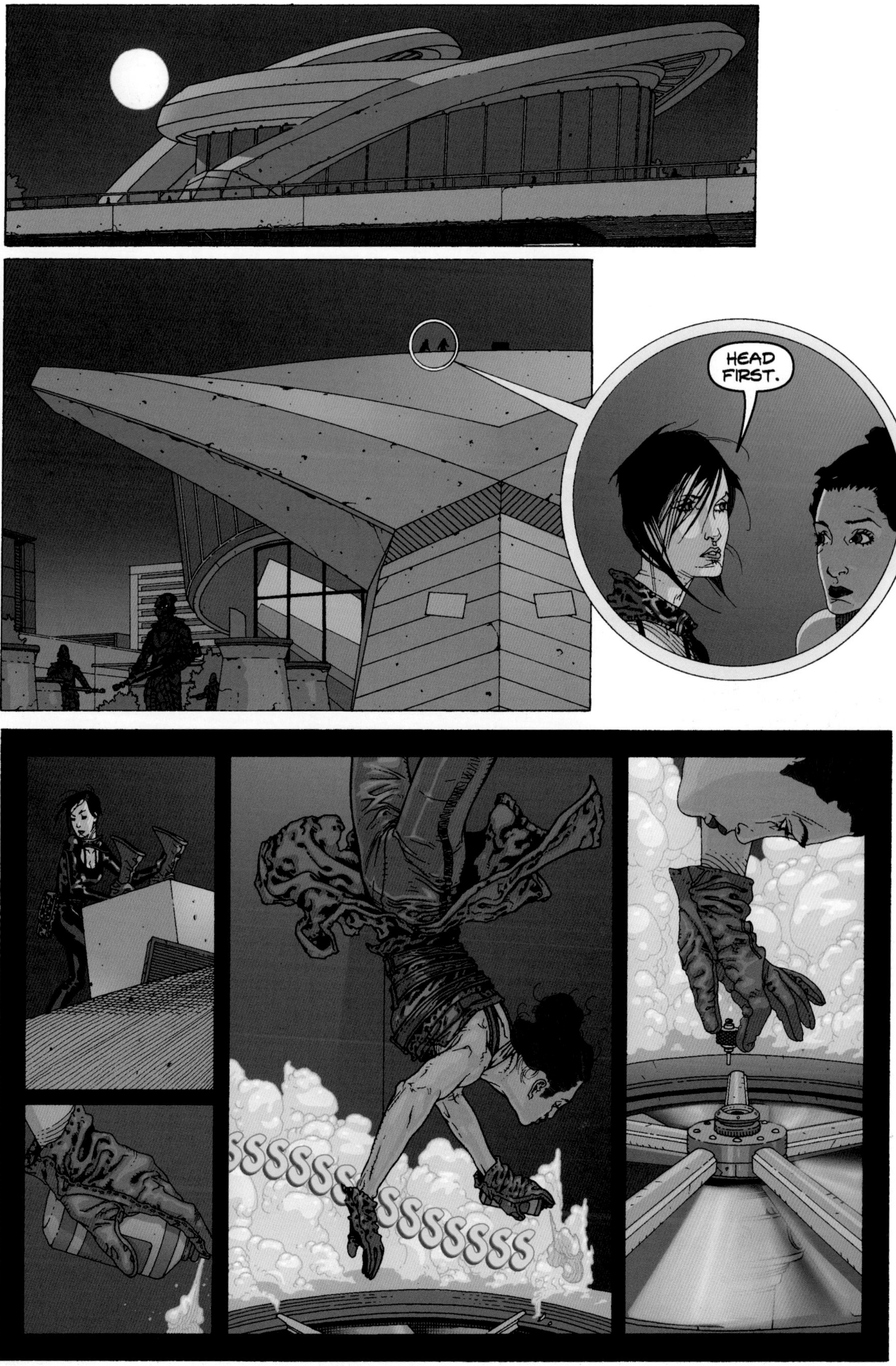
HEAD FIRST.
SSSSSSSSSSSSSSSSS

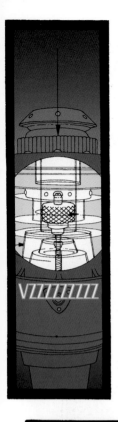

VZZZZZZZZ

WHRRRR-CH-CH-CHAK- CH-M-THM-TH-THUMP-THUMP- THMP- THMP

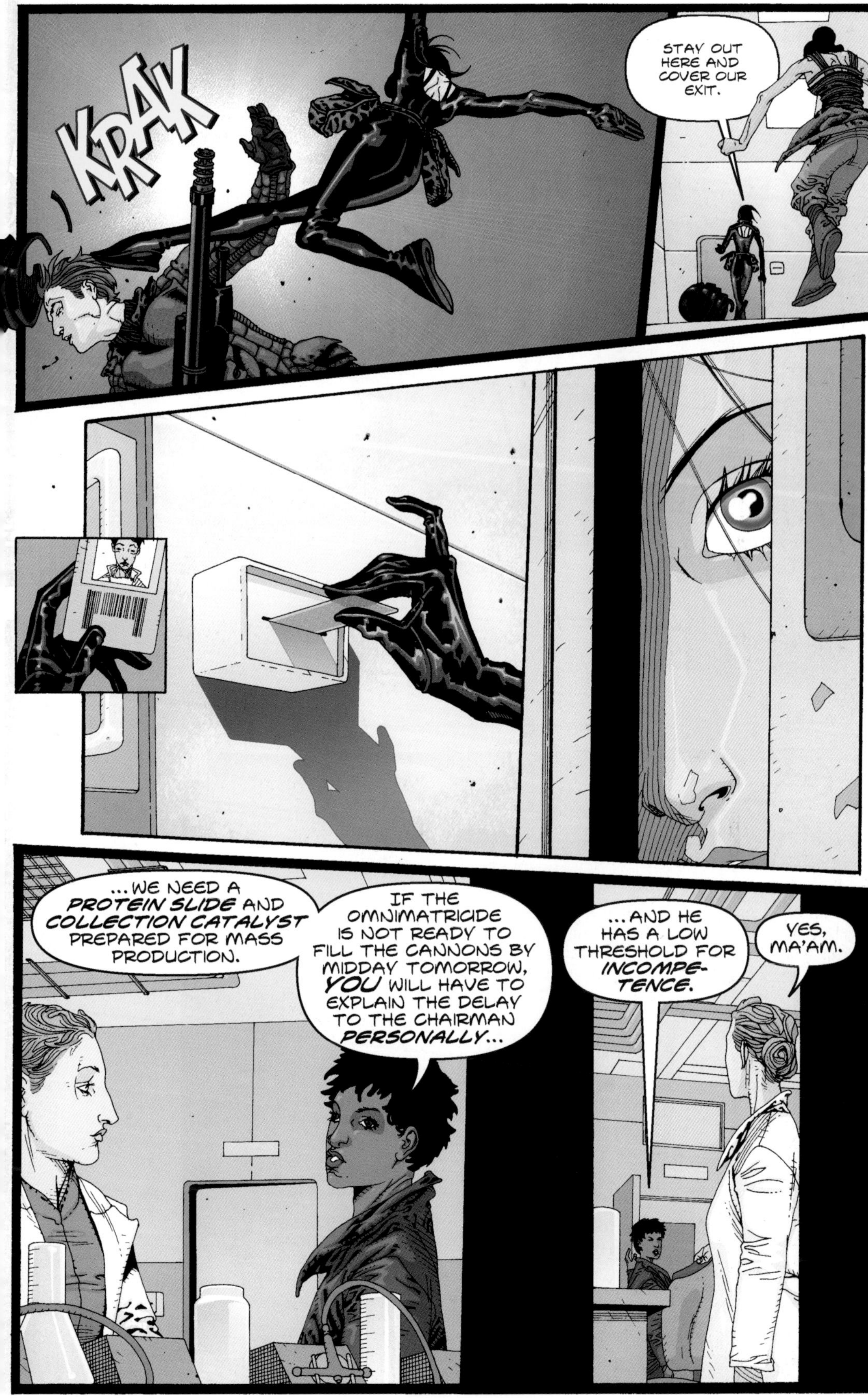
KRAK
STAY OUT HERE AND COVER OUR EXIT.
...WE NEED A PROTEIN SLIDE AND COLLECTION CATALYST PREPARED FOR MASS PRODUCTION.
IF THE OMNIMATRICIDE IS NOT READY TO FILL THE CANNONS BY MIDDAY TOMORROW, YOU WILL HAVE TO EXPLAIN THE DELAY TO THE CHAIRMAN PERSONALLY...
...AND HE HAS A LOW THRESHOLD FOR INCOMPE-TENCE.
YES, MA'AM.

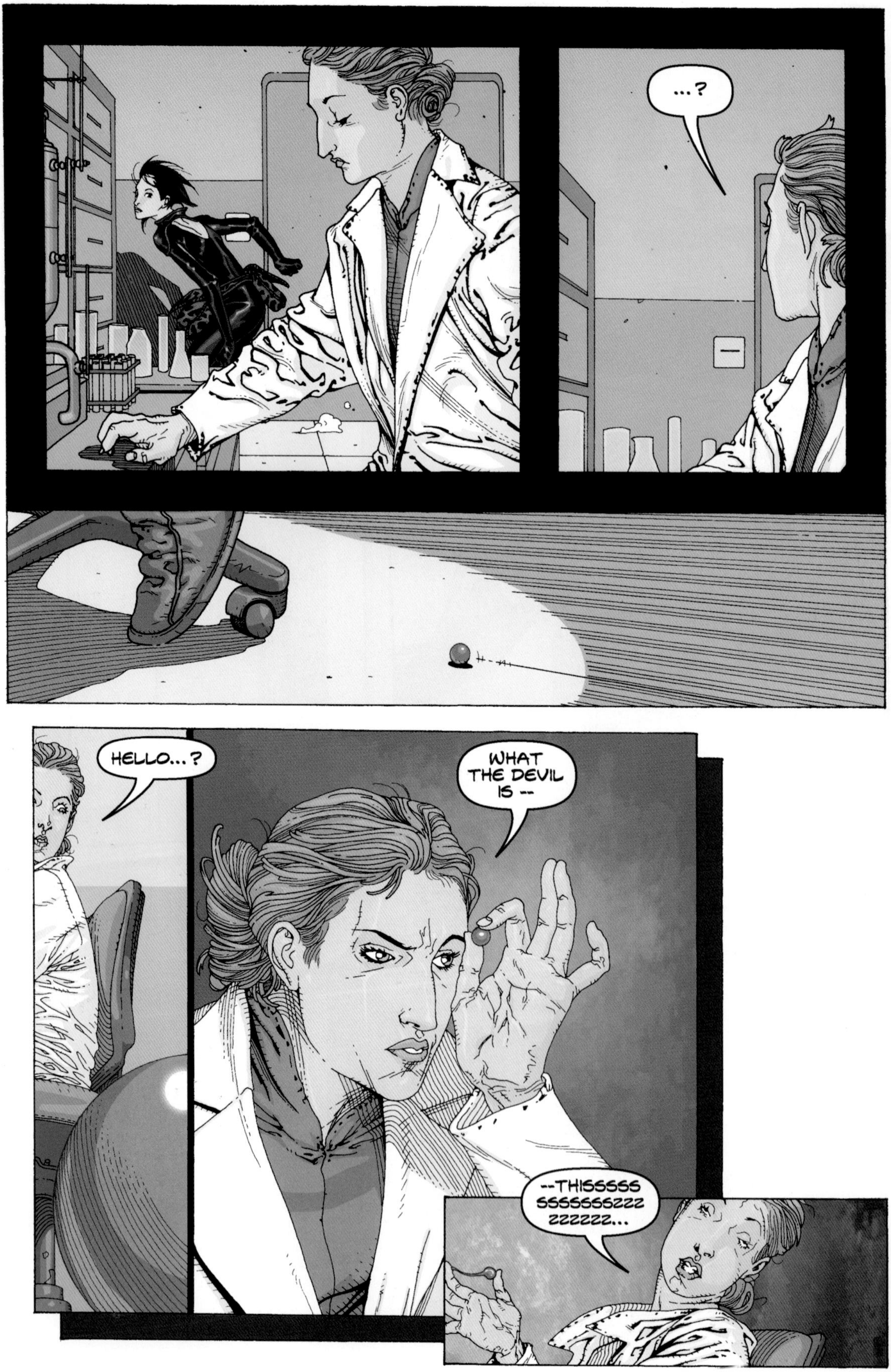
...?
HELLO...?
WHAT THE DEVIL IS --
--THISSSSS SSSSSSSZZZ ZZZZZZ...

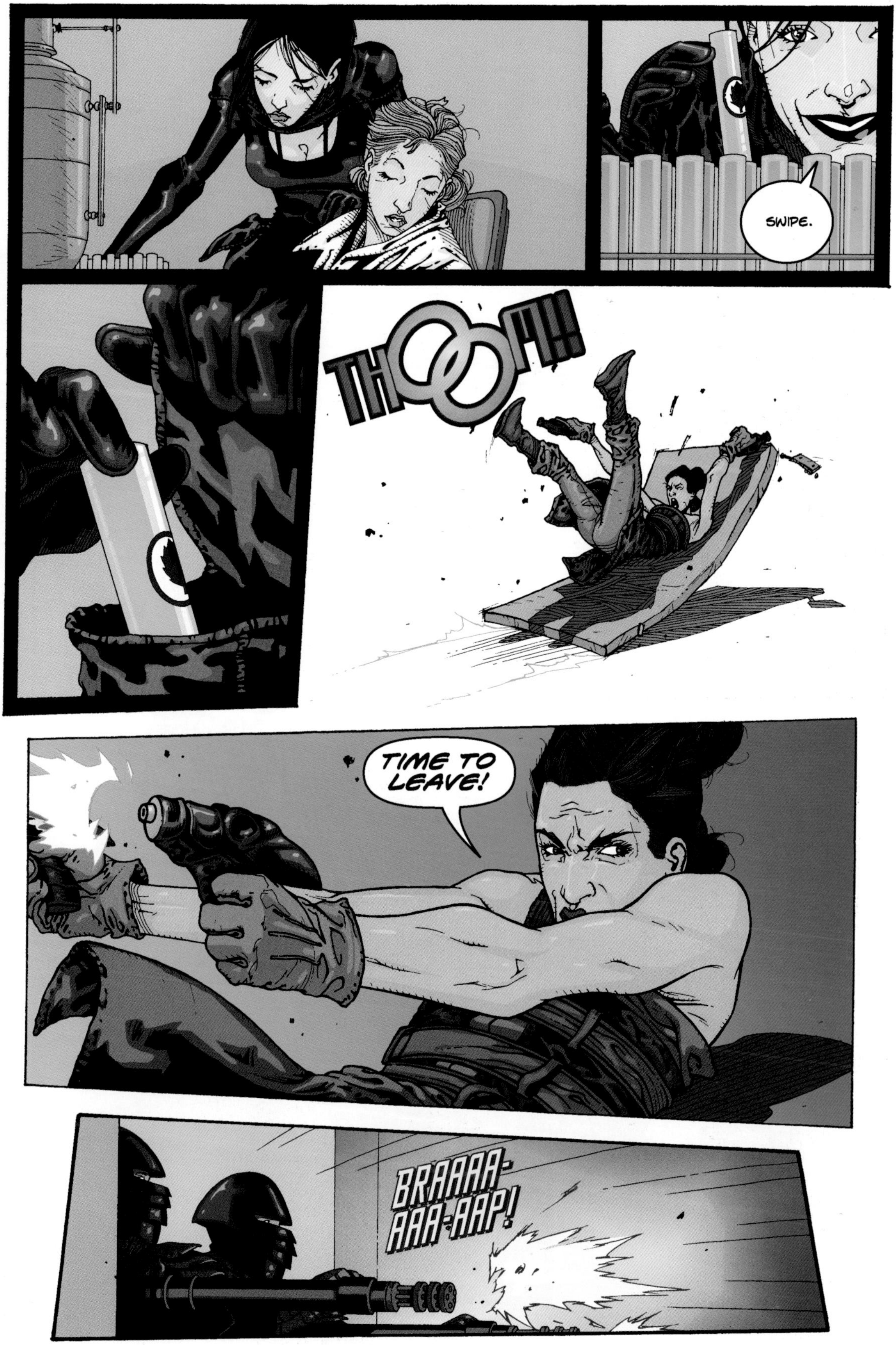
SWIPE.
THOOM!!
TIME TO LEAVE!
BRAAAA-AAA-AAP!

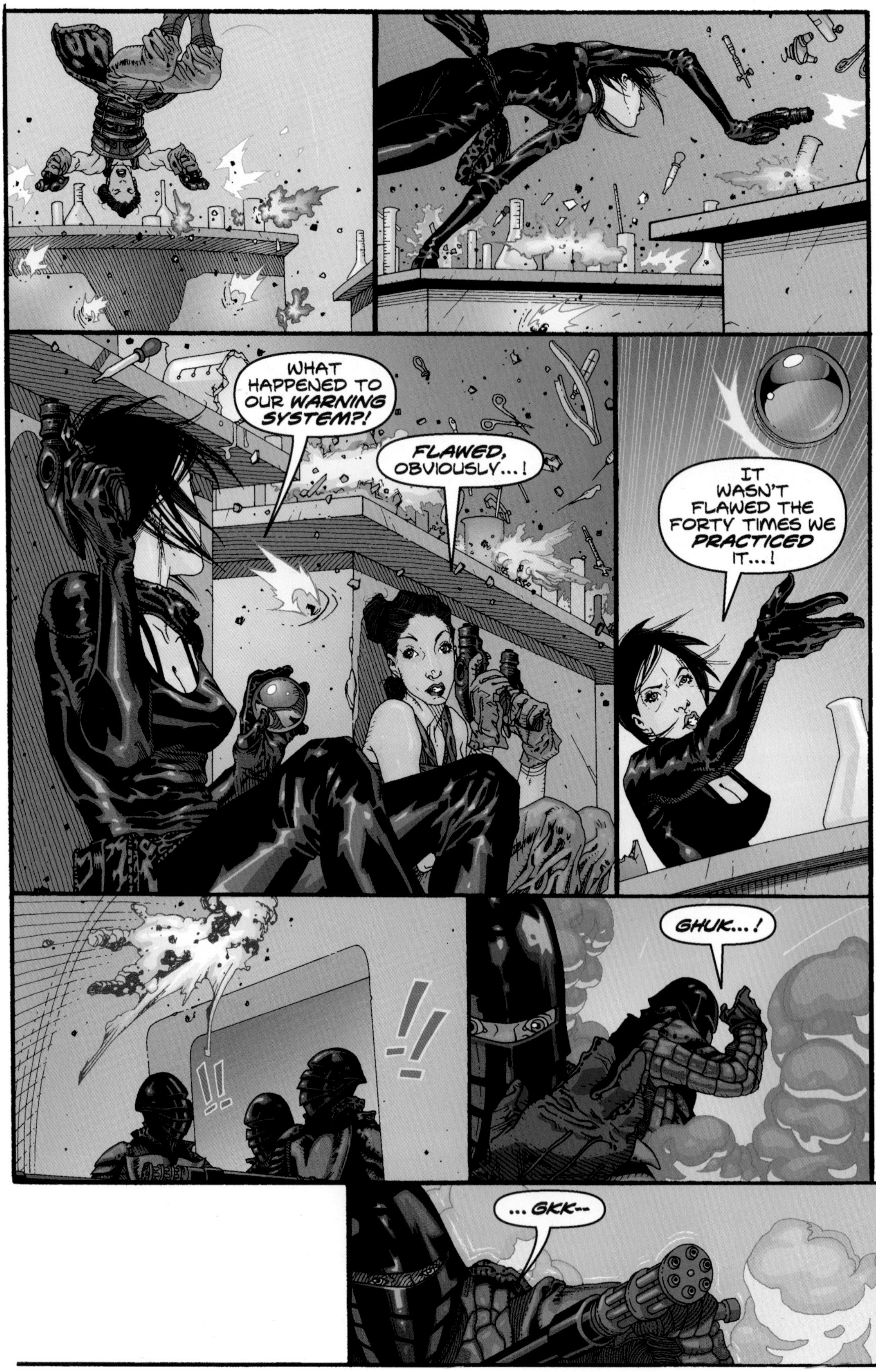
WHAT HAPPENED TO OUR WARNING SYSTEM?!
FLAWED, OBVIOUSLY...!
IT WASN'T FLAWED THE FORTY TIMES WE PRACTICED IT...!
GHUK...!
...GKK--

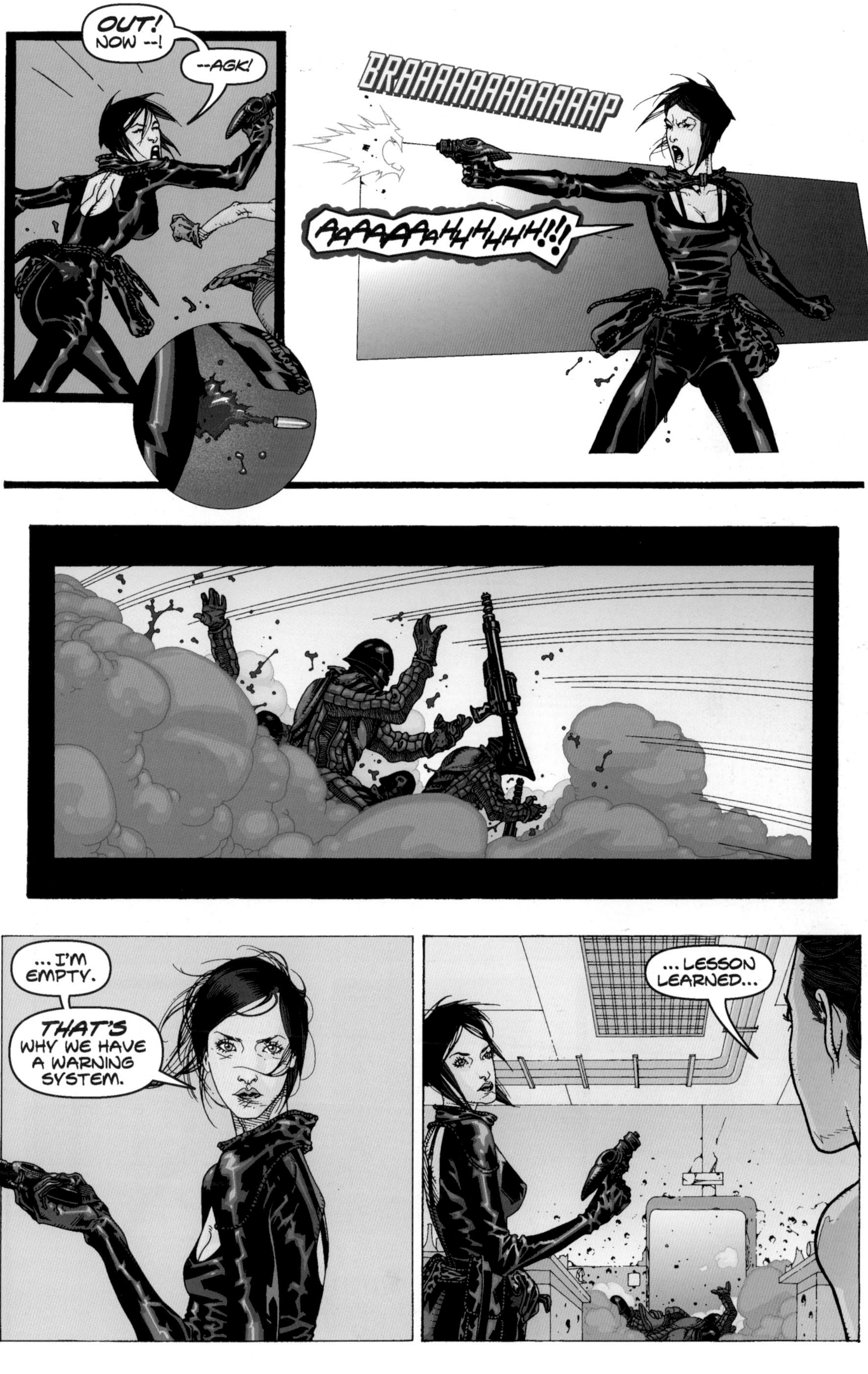
OUT! NOW --!
--AGK!
BRAAAAAAAAAAAAAP
AAAAAAAHHHHHH!!!
... I'M EMPTY.
THAT'S WHY WE HAVE A WARNING SYSTEM.
... LESSON LEARNED...

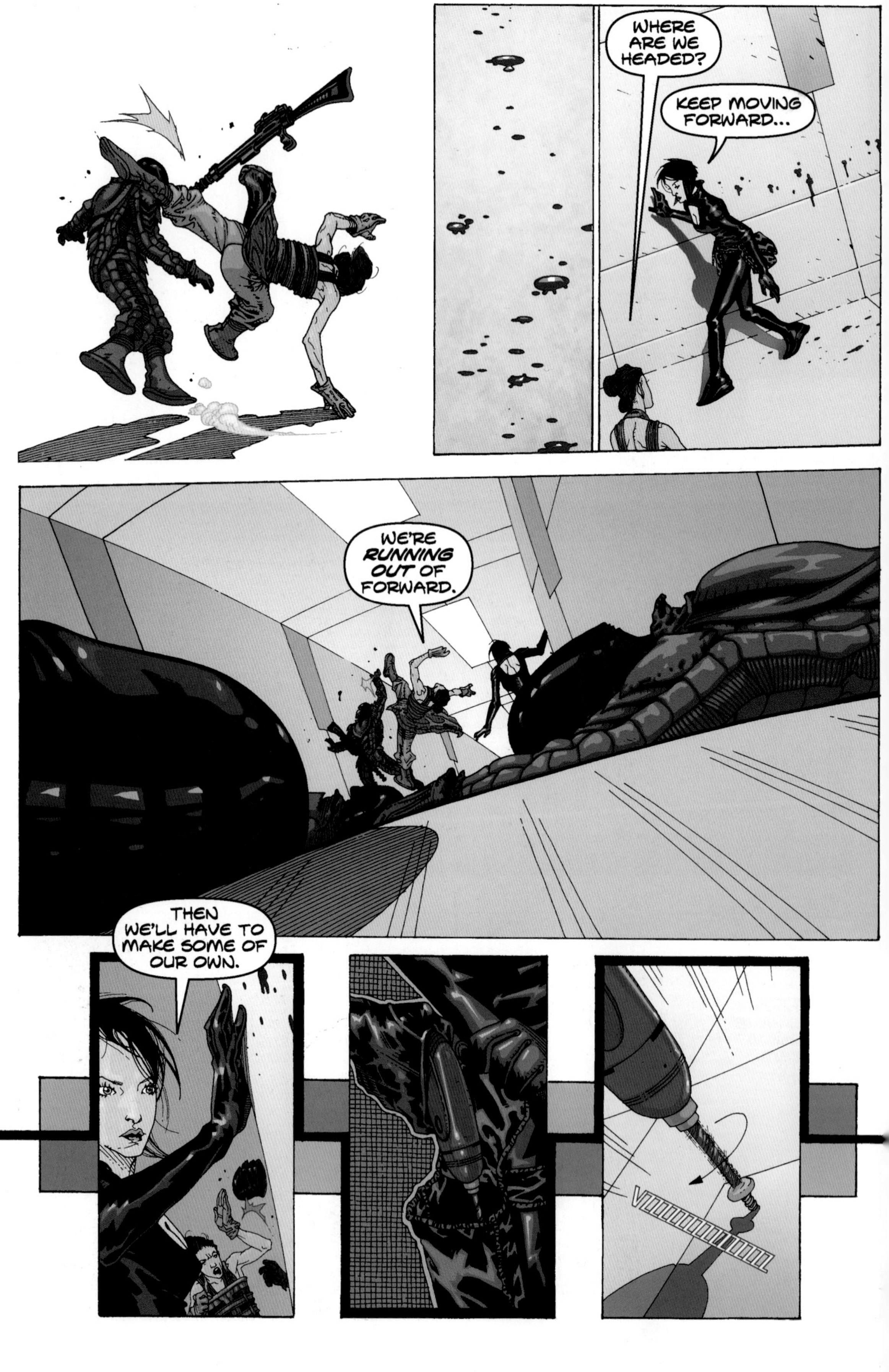
WHERE ARE WE HEADED?
KEEP MOVING FORWARD...
WE'RE *RUNNING OUT* OF FORWARD.
THEN WE'LL HAVE TO MAKE SOME OF OUR OWN.
VZZZZZZZZZZZZZ

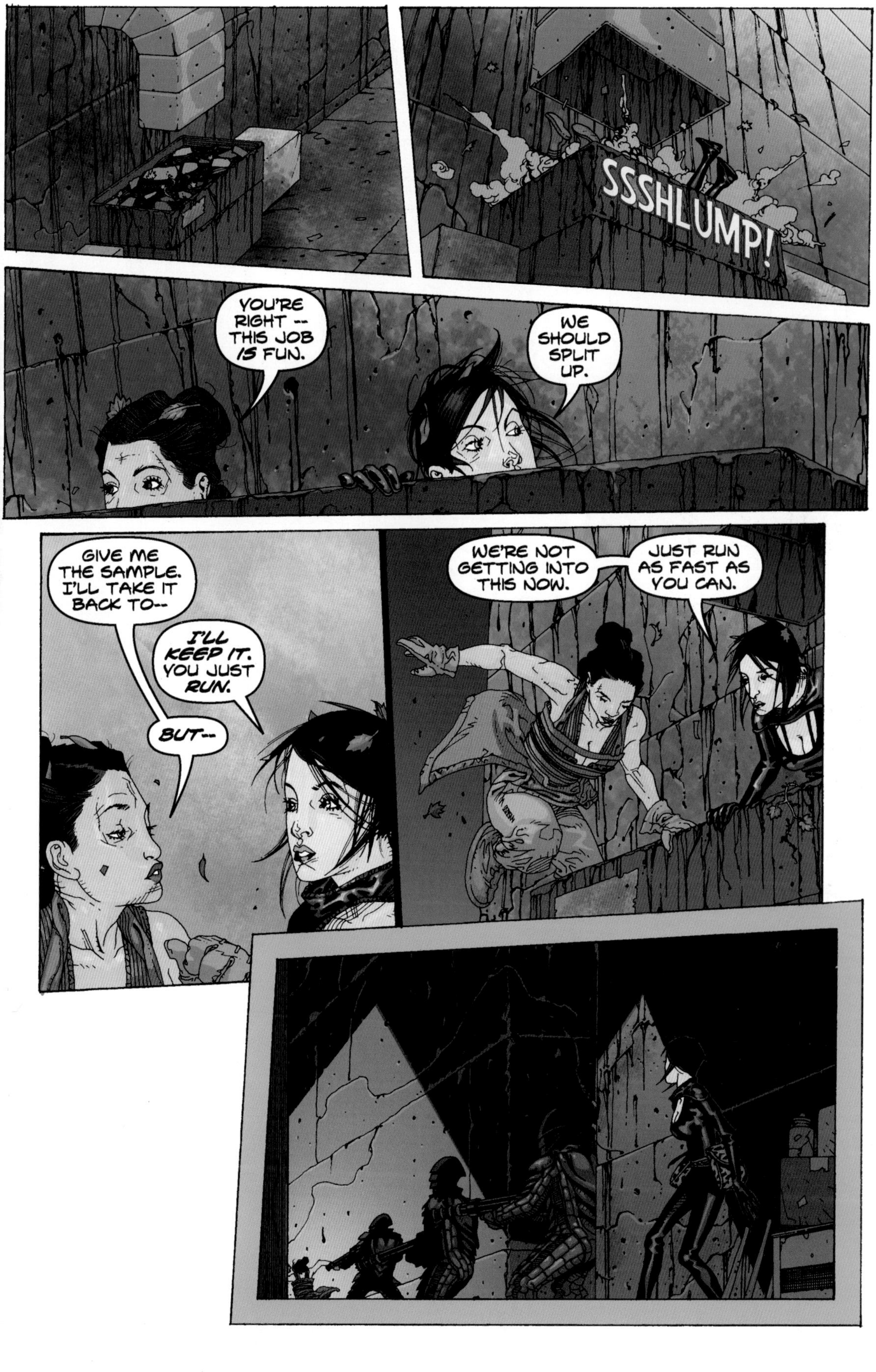
SSSHLUMP!
YOU'RE RIGHT -- THIS JOB IS FUN.
WE SHOULD SPLIT UP.
GIVE ME THE SAMPLE. I'LL TAKE IT BACK TO--
I'LL KEEP IT. YOU JUST RUN.
BUT--
WE'RE NOT GETTING INTO THIS NOW.
JUST RUN AS FAST AS YOU CAN.

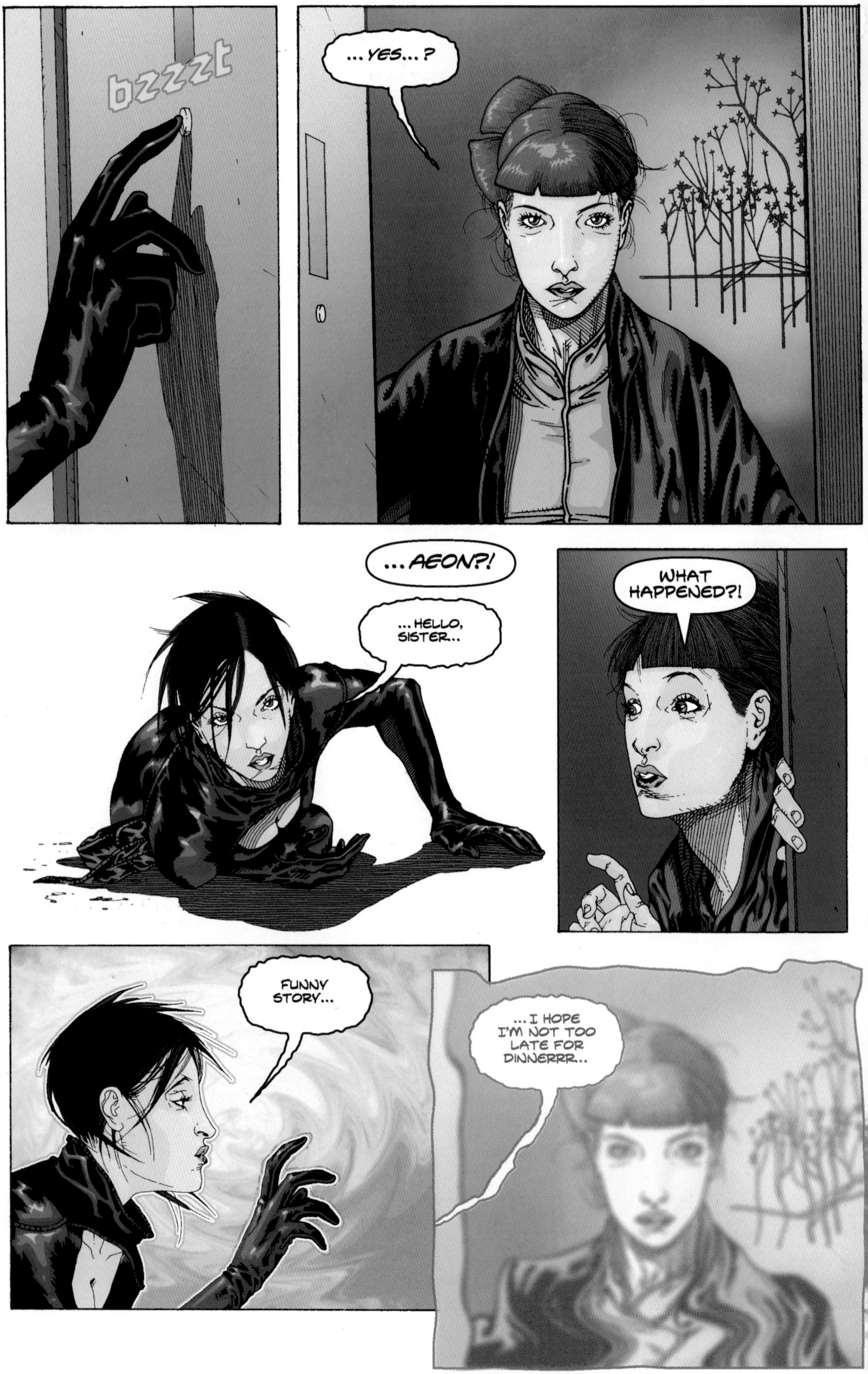
bzzzt
...YES...?
...AEON?!
...HELLO, SISTER...
WHAT HAPPENED?!
FUNNY STORY...
...I HOPE I'M NOT TOO LATE FOR DINNERRR...

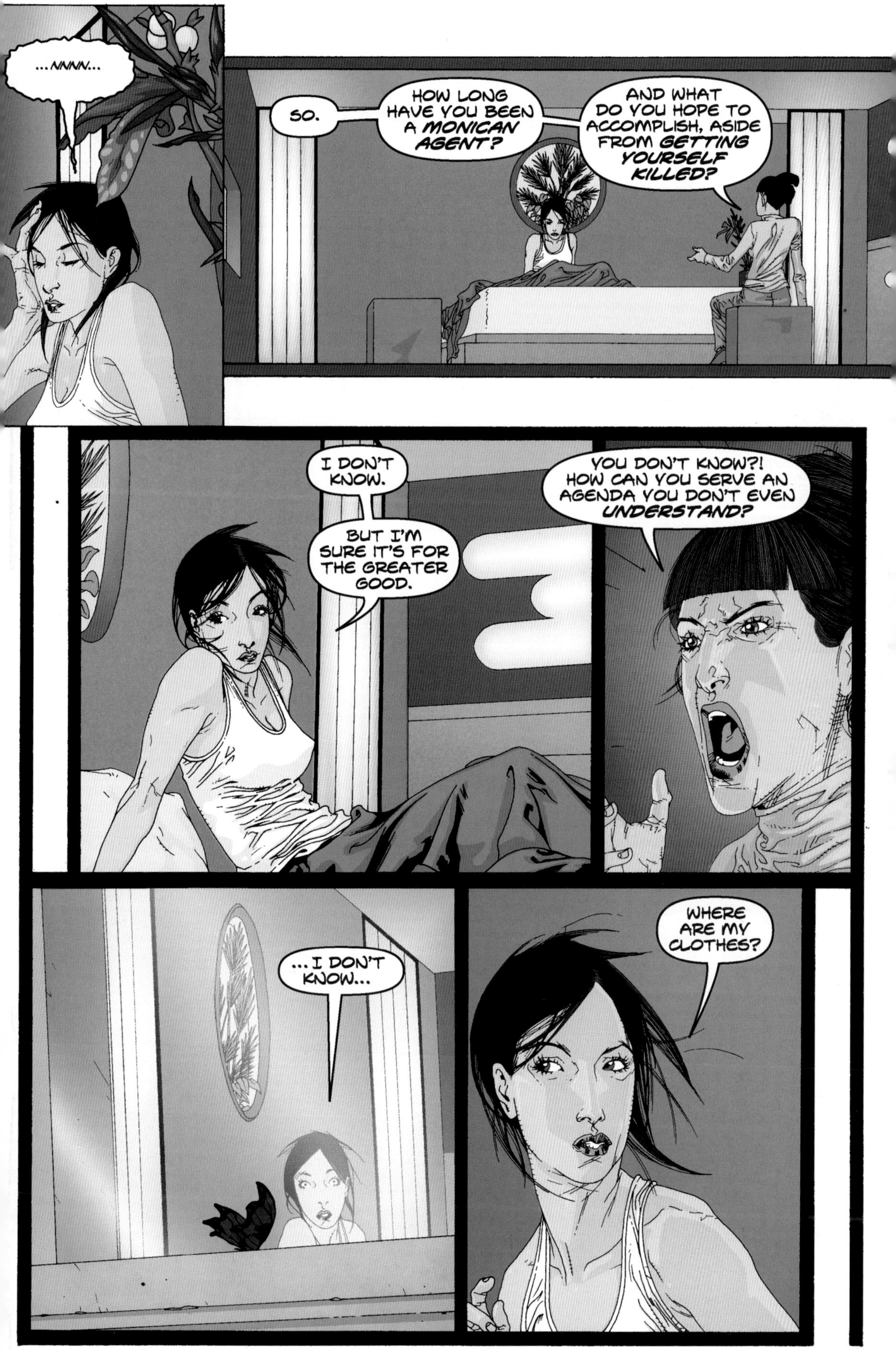
...NNNN...
SO.
HOW LONG HAVE YOU BEEN A MONICAN AGENT?
AND WHAT DO YOU HOPE TO ACCOMPLISH, ASIDE FROM GETTING YOURSELF KILLED?
I DON'T KNOW.
BUT I'M SURE IT'S FOR THE GREATER GOOD.
YOU DON'T KNOW?! HOW CAN YOU SERVE AN AGENDA YOU DON'T EVEN UNDERSTAND?
...I DON'T KNOW...
WHERE ARE MY CLOTHES?

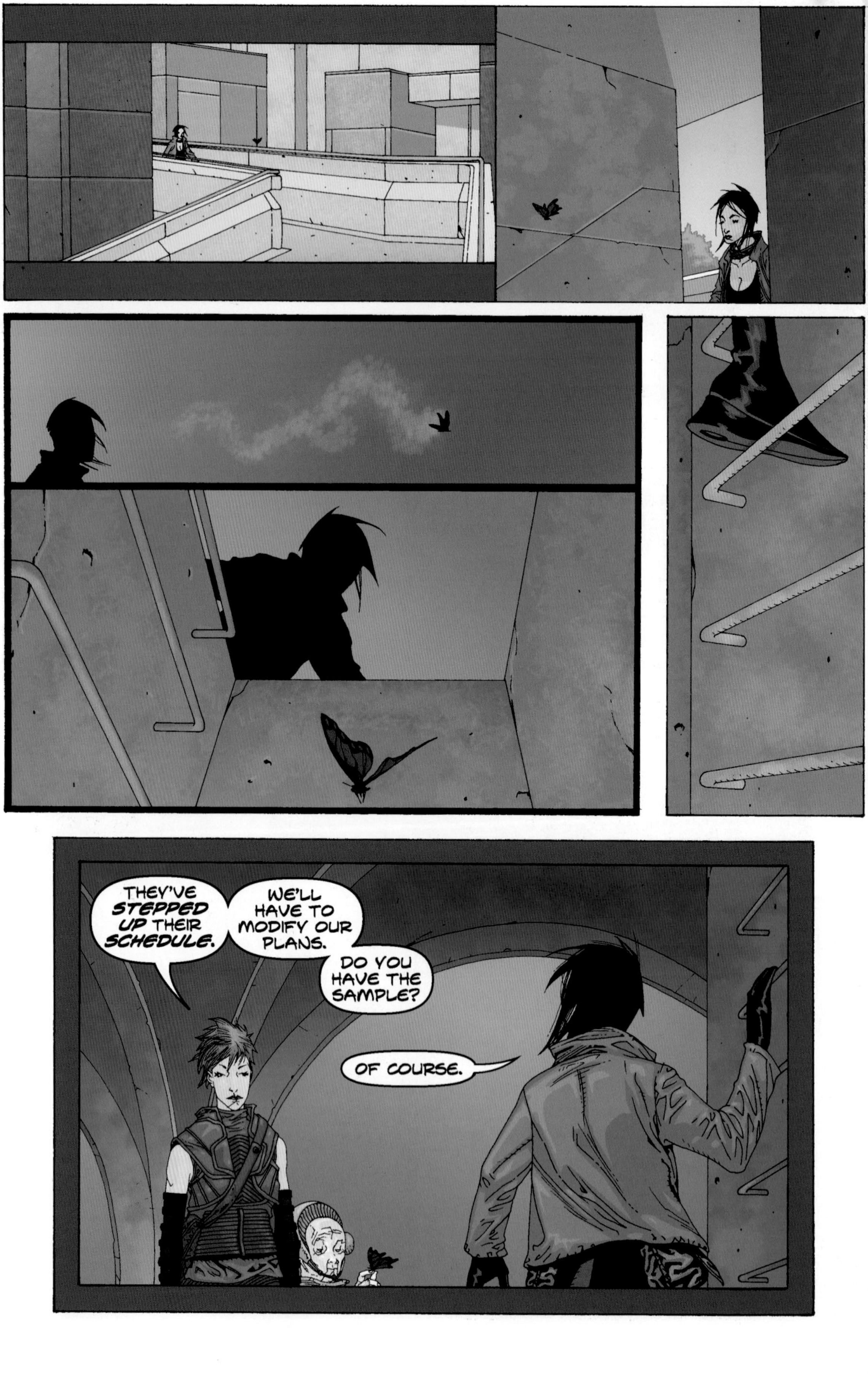

THEY'VE *STEPPED UP* THEIR *SCHEDULE*.
WE'LL HAVE TO MODIFY OUR PLANS.
DO YOU HAVE THE SAMPLE?
OF COURSE.

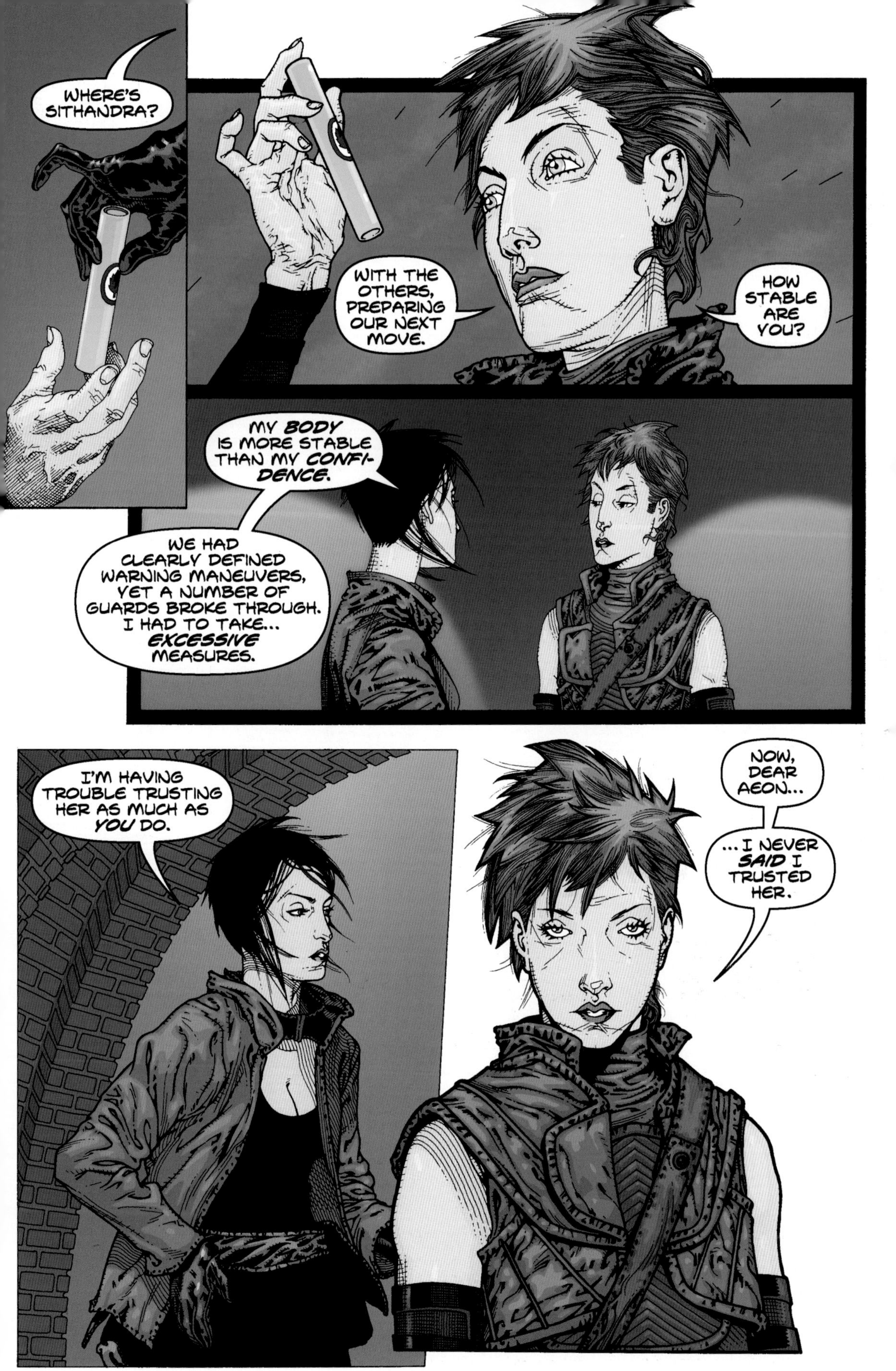
WHERE'S SITHANDRA?
WITH THE OTHERS, PREPARING OUR NEXT MOVE.
HOW STABLE ARE YOU?
MY BODY IS MORE STABLE THAN MY CONFI-DENCE.
WE HAD CLEARLY DEFINED WARNING MANEUVERS, YET A NUMBER OF GUARDS BROKE THROUGH. I HAD TO TAKE... EXCESSIVE MEASURES.
I'M HAVING TROUBLE TRUSTING HER AS MUCH AS YOU DO.
NOW, DEAR AEON...
...I NEVER SAID I TRUSTED HER.

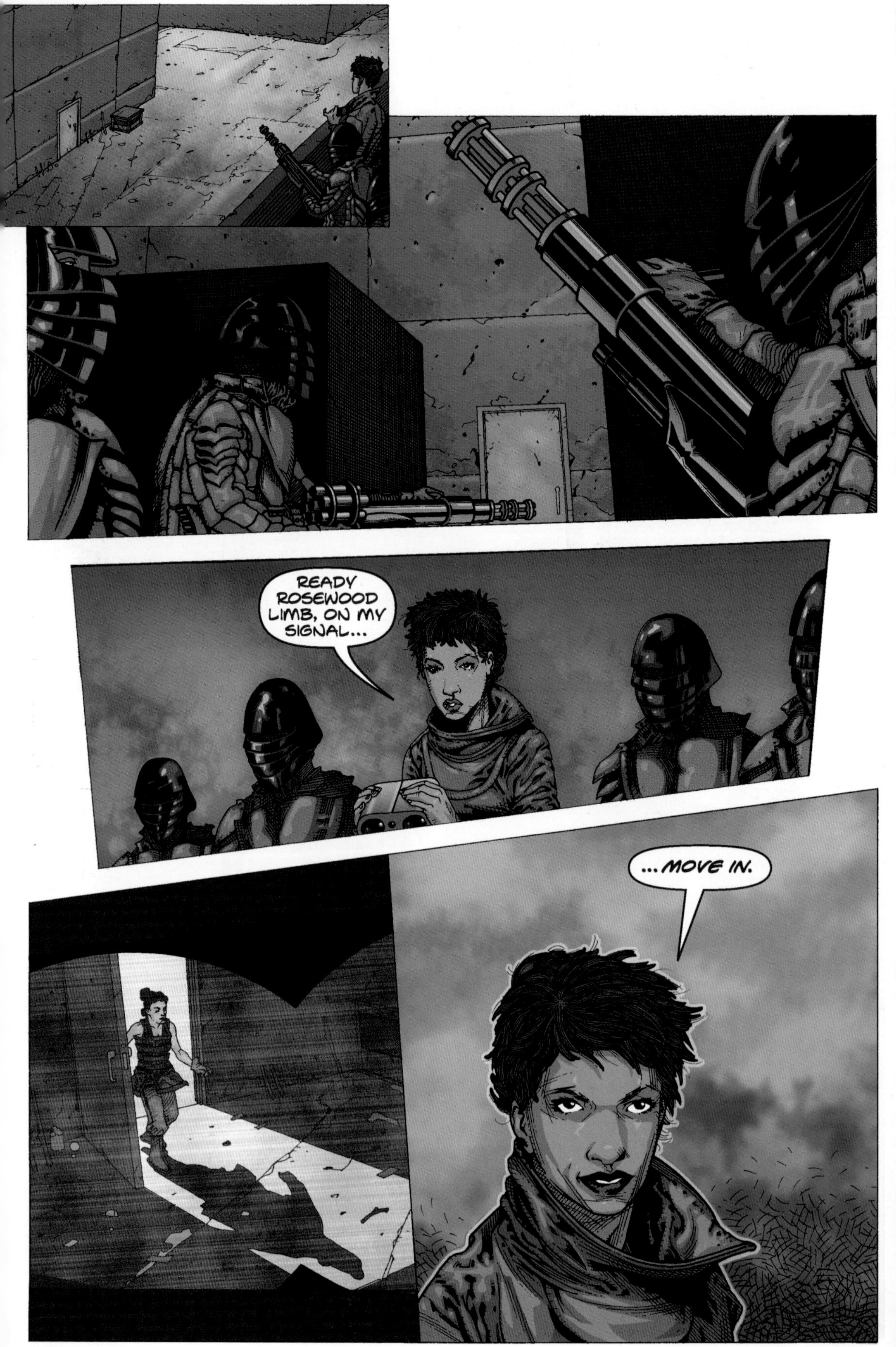
READY ROSEWOOD LIMB, ON MY SIGNAL...
...MOVE IN.

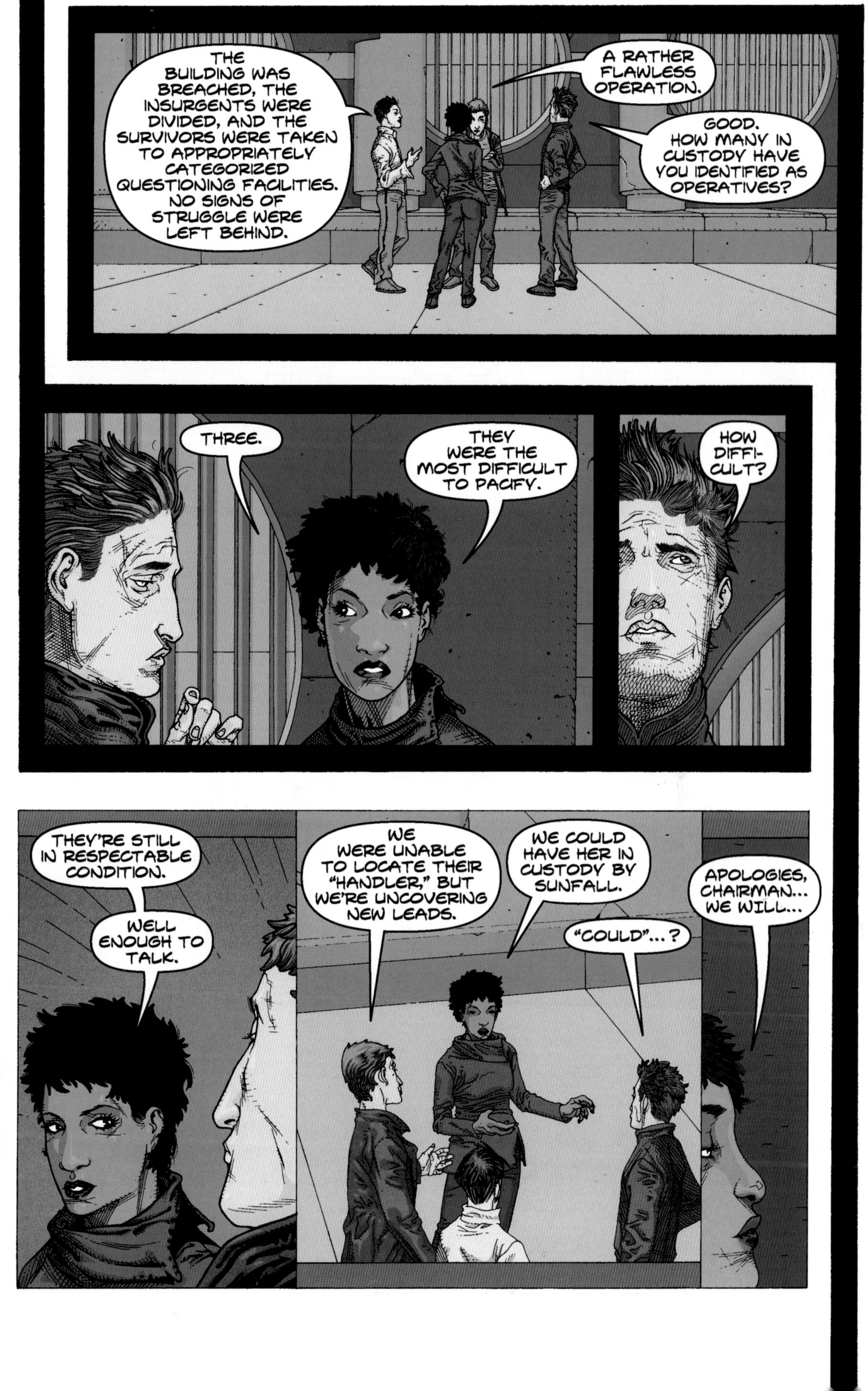
THE BUILDING WAS BREACHED, THE INSURGENTS WERE DIVIDED, AND THE SURVIVORS WERE TAKEN TO APPROPRIATELY CATEGORIZED QUESTIONING FACILITIES. NO SIGNS OF STRUGGLE WERE LEFT BEHIND.
A RATHER FLAWLESS OPERATION.
GOOD. HOW MANY IN CUSTODY HAVE YOU IDENTIFIED AS OPERATIVES?
THREE.
THEY WERE THE MOST DIFFICULT TO PACIFY.
HOW DIFFI-CULT?
THEY'RE STILL IN RESPECTABLE CONDITION.
WELL ENOUGH TO TALK.
WE WERE UNABLE TO LOCATE THEIR "HANDLER," BUT WE'RE UNCOVERING NEW LEADS.
WE COULD HAVE HER IN CUSTODY BY SUNFALL.
"COULD"...?
APOLOGIES, CHAIRMAN... WE WILL...

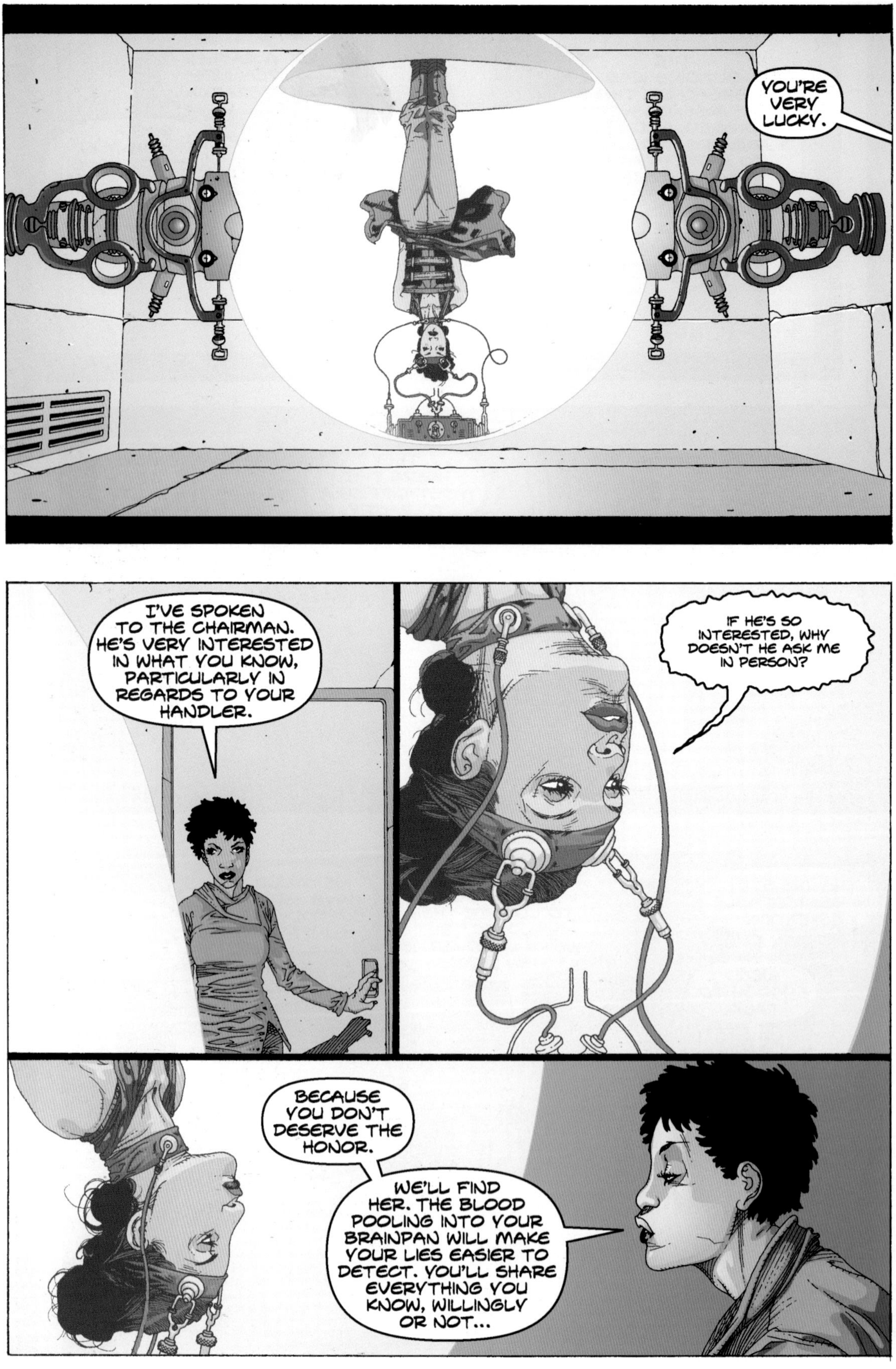
YOU'RE VERY LUCKY.
I'VE SPOKEN TO THE CHAIRMAN. HE'S VERY INTERESTED IN WHAT YOU KNOW, PARTICULARLY IN REGARDS TO YOUR HANDLER.
IF HE'S SO INTERESTED, WHY DOESN'T HE ASK ME IN PERSON?
BECAUSE YOU DON'T DESERVE THE HONOR.
WE'LL FIND HER. THE BLOOD POOLING INTO YOUR BRAINPAN WILL MAKE YOUR LIES EASIER TO DETECT. YOU'LL SHARE EVERYTHING YOU KNOW, WILLINGLY OR NOT...

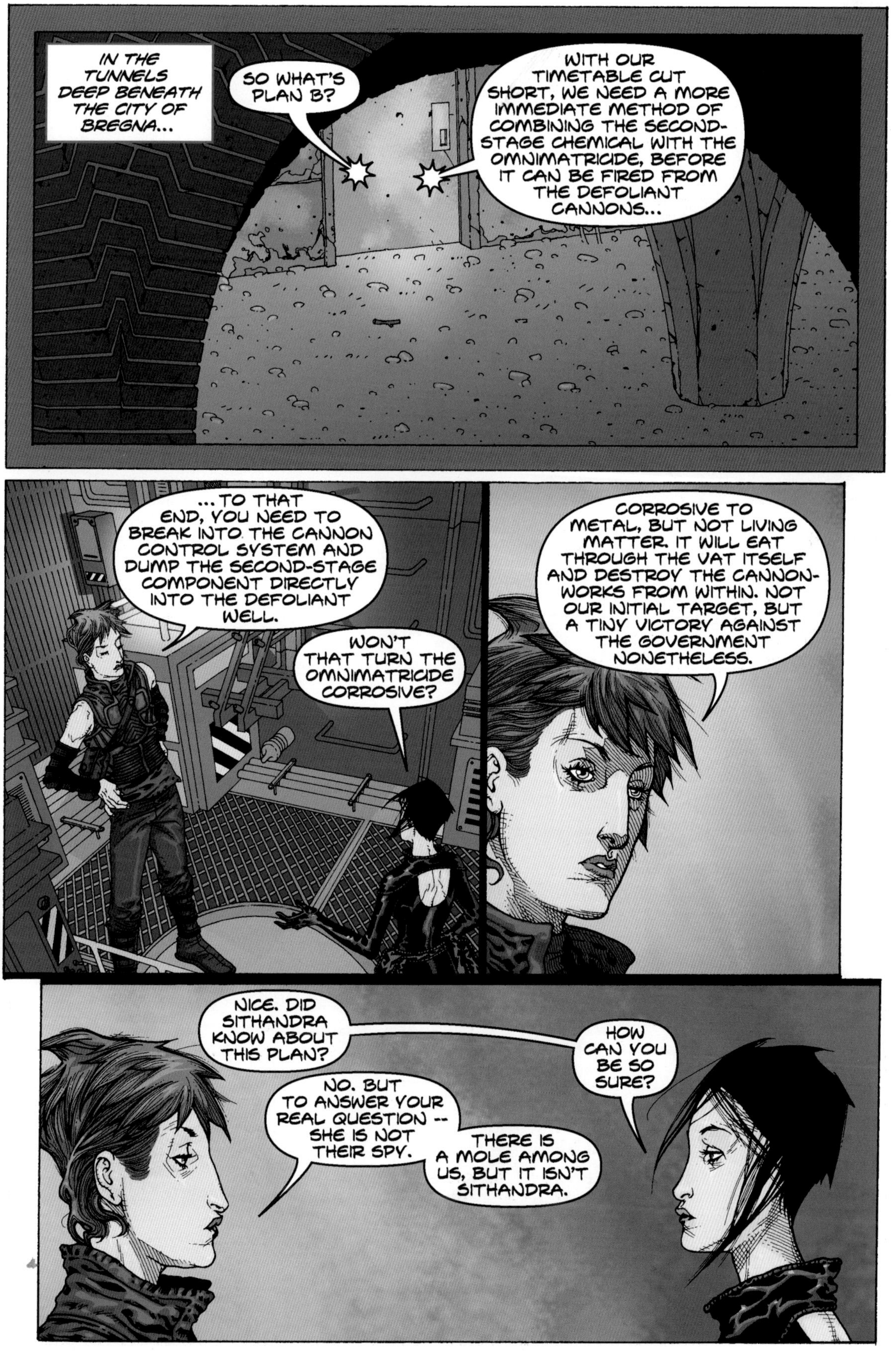
IN THE TUNNELS DEEP BENEATH THE CITY OF BREGNA...
SO WHAT'S PLAN B?
WITH OUR TIMETABLE CUT SHORT, WE NEED A MORE IMMEDIATE METHOD OF COMBINING THE SECOND-STAGE CHEMICAL WITH THE OMNIMATRICIDE, BEFORE IT CAN BE FIRED FROM THE DEFOLIANT CANNONS...
...TO THAT END, YOU NEED TO BREAK INTO THE CANNON CONTROL SYSTEM AND DUMP THE SECOND-STAGE COMPONENT DIRECTLY INTO THE DEFOLIANT WELL.
WON'T THAT TURN THE OMNIMATRICIDE CORROSIVE?
CORROSIVE TO METAL, BUT NOT LIVING MATTER. IT WILL EAT THROUGH THE VAT ITSELF AND DESTROY THE CANNON-WORKS FROM WITHIN. NOT OUR INITIAL TARGET, BUT A TINY VICTORY AGAINST THE GOVERNMENT NONETHELESS.
NICE. DID SITHANDRA KNOW ABOUT THIS PLAN?
NO. BUT TO ANSWER YOUR REAL QUESTION -- SHE IS NOT THEIR SPY.
HOW CAN YOU BE SO SURE?
THERE IS A MOLE AMONG US, BUT IT ISN'T SITHANDRA.

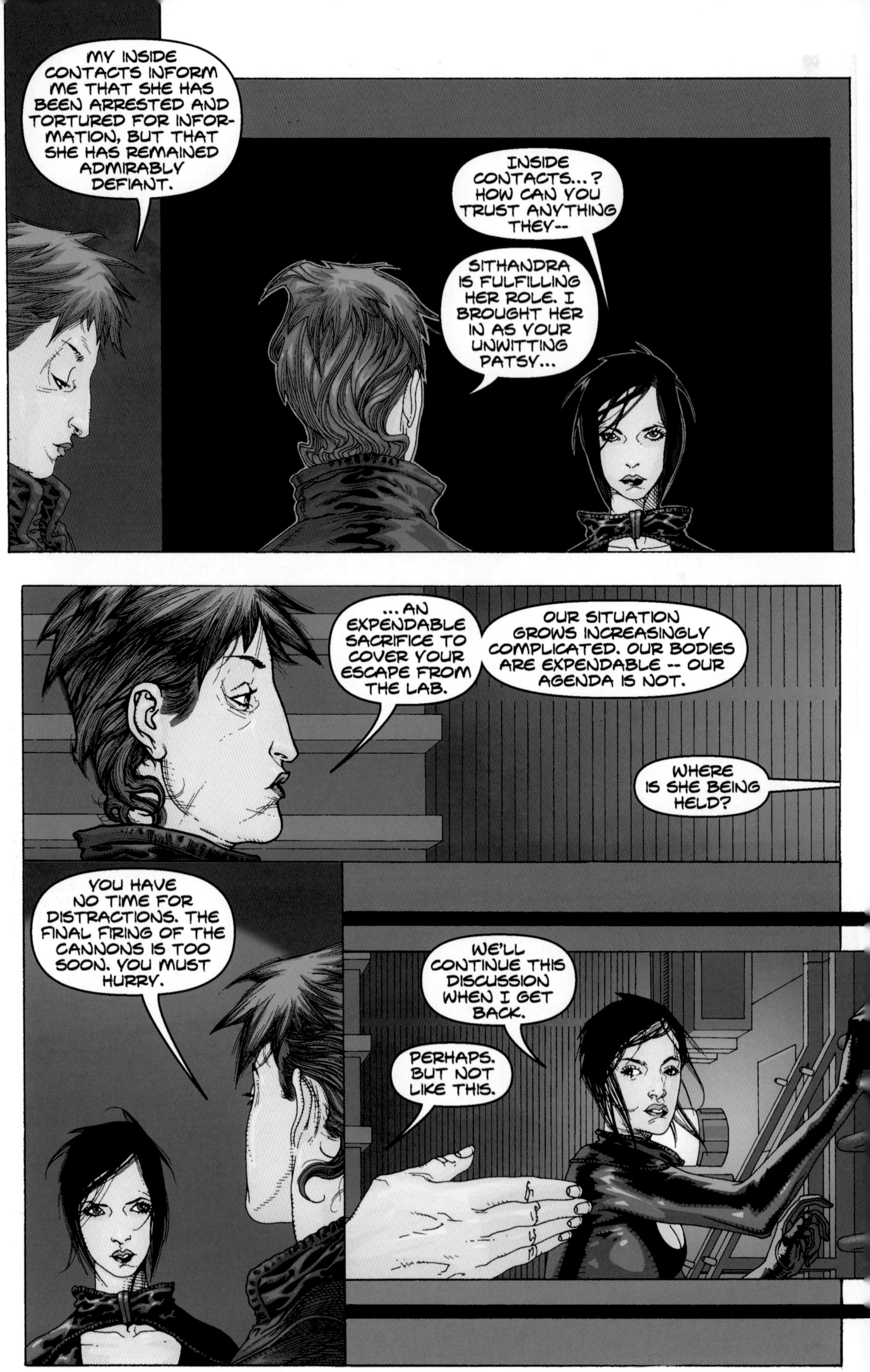
MY INSIDE CONTACTS INFORM ME THAT SHE HAS BEEN ARRESTED AND TORTURED FOR INFORMATION, BUT THAT SHE HAS REMAINED ADMIRABLY DEFIANT.
INSIDE CONTACTS...? HOW CAN YOU TRUST ANYTHING THEY--
SITHANDRA IS FULFILLING HER ROLE. I BROUGHT HER IN AS YOUR UNWITTING PATSY...
...AN EXPENDABLE SACRIFICE TO COVER YOUR ESCAPE FROM THE LAB.
OUR SITUATION GROWS INCREASINGLY COMPLICATED. OUR BODIES ARE EXPENDABLE -- OUR AGENDA IS NOT.
WHERE IS SHE BEING HELD?
YOU HAVE NO TIME FOR DISTRACTIONS. THE FINAL FIRING OF THE CANNONS IS TOO SOON. YOU MUST HURRY.
WE'LL CONTINUE THIS DISCUSSION WHEN I GET BACK.
PERHAPS. BUT NOT LIKE THIS.

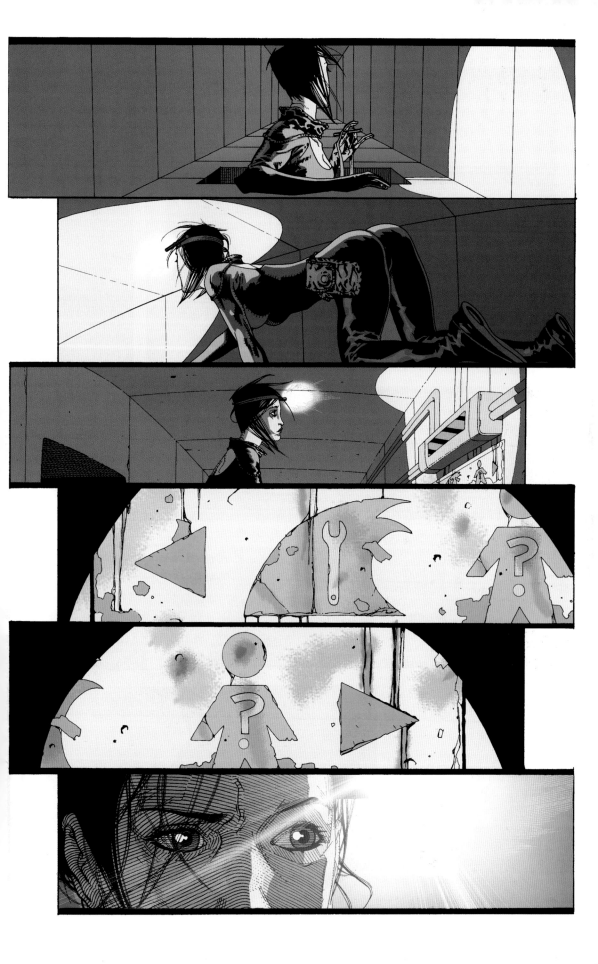

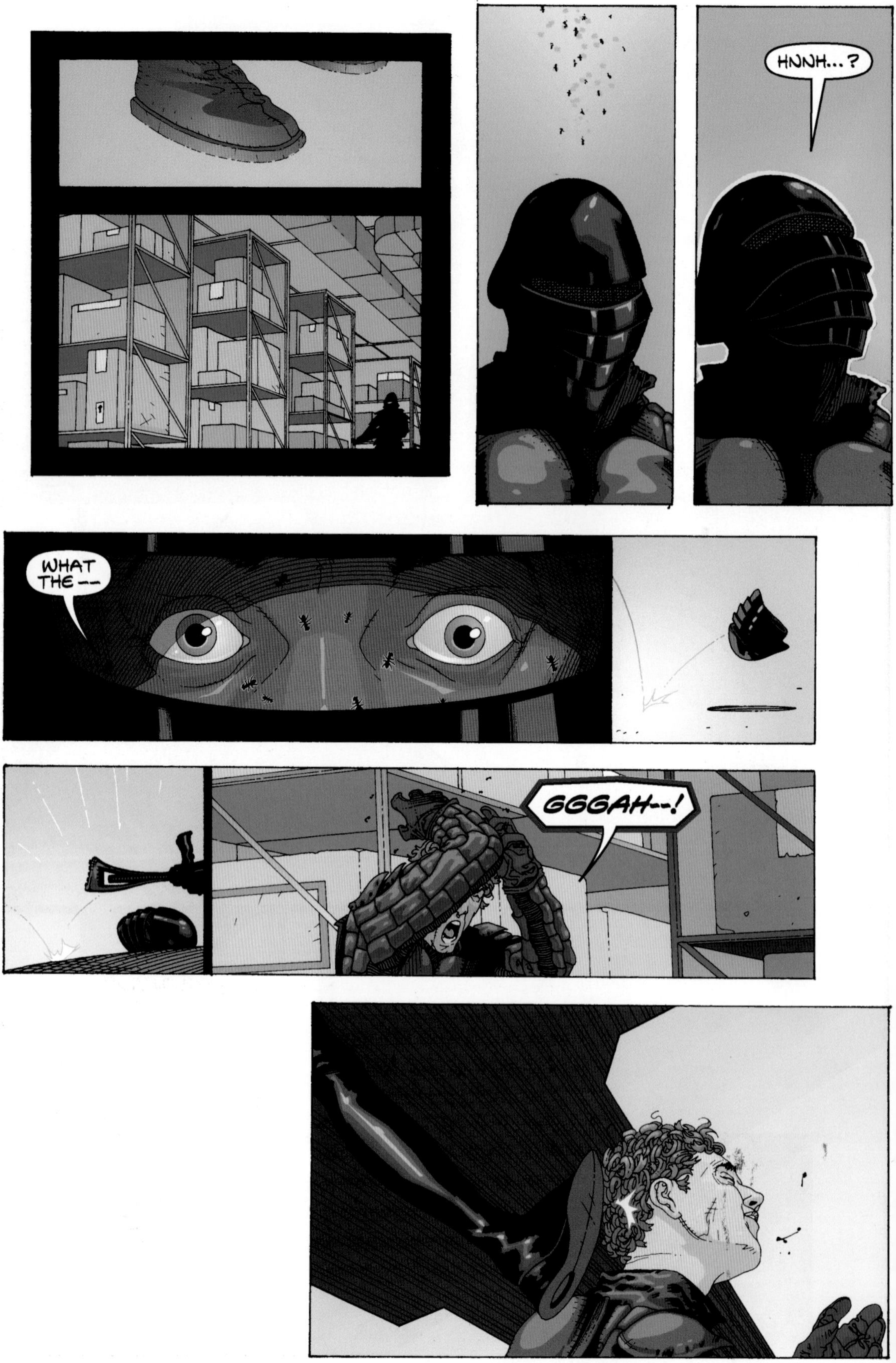
HNNH...?
WHAT THE--
GGGAH--!

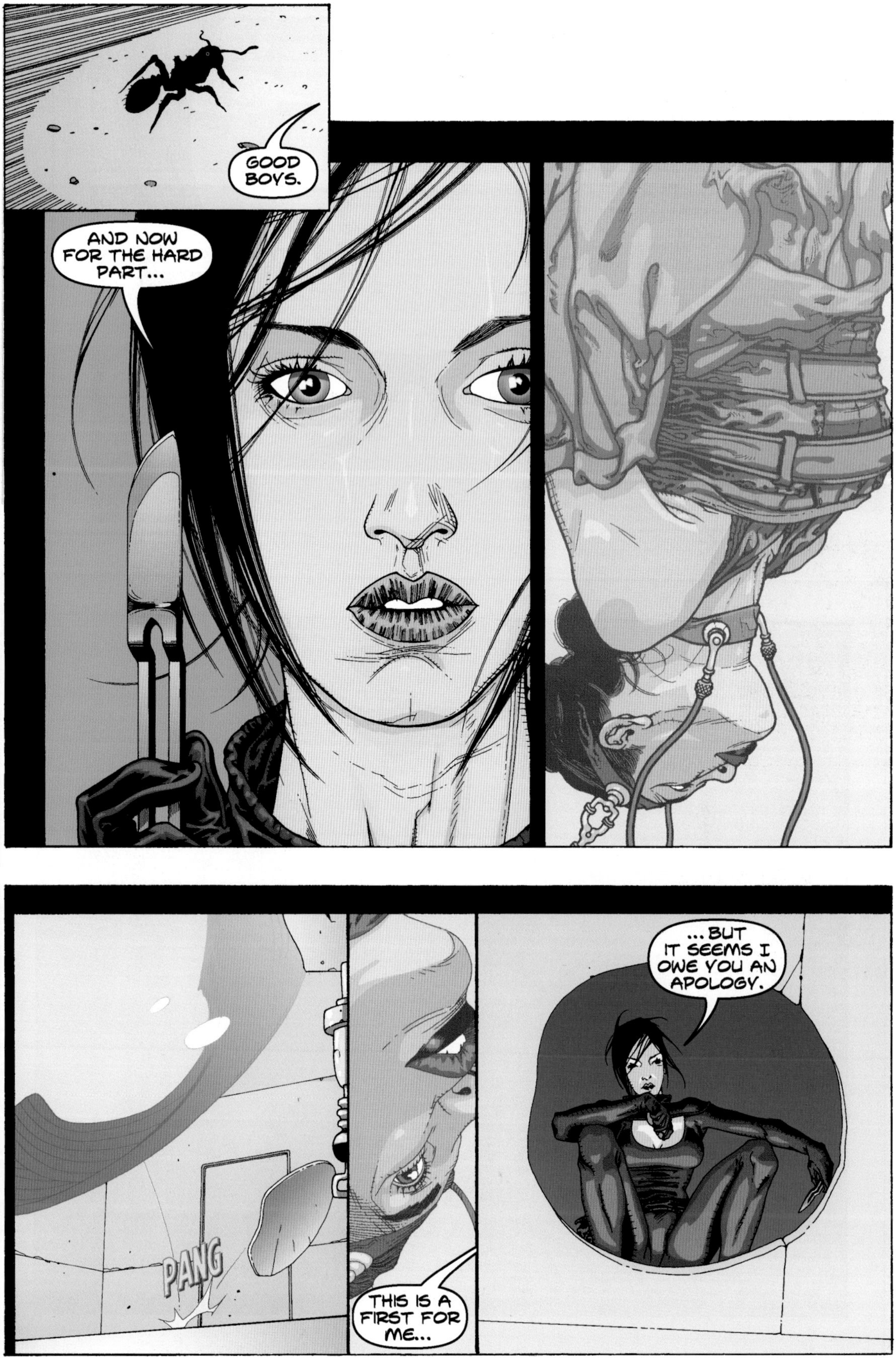
GOOD BOYS.
AND NOW FOR THE HARD PART...
PANG
THIS IS A FIRST FOR ME...
...BUT IT SEEMS I OWE YOU AN APOLOGY.

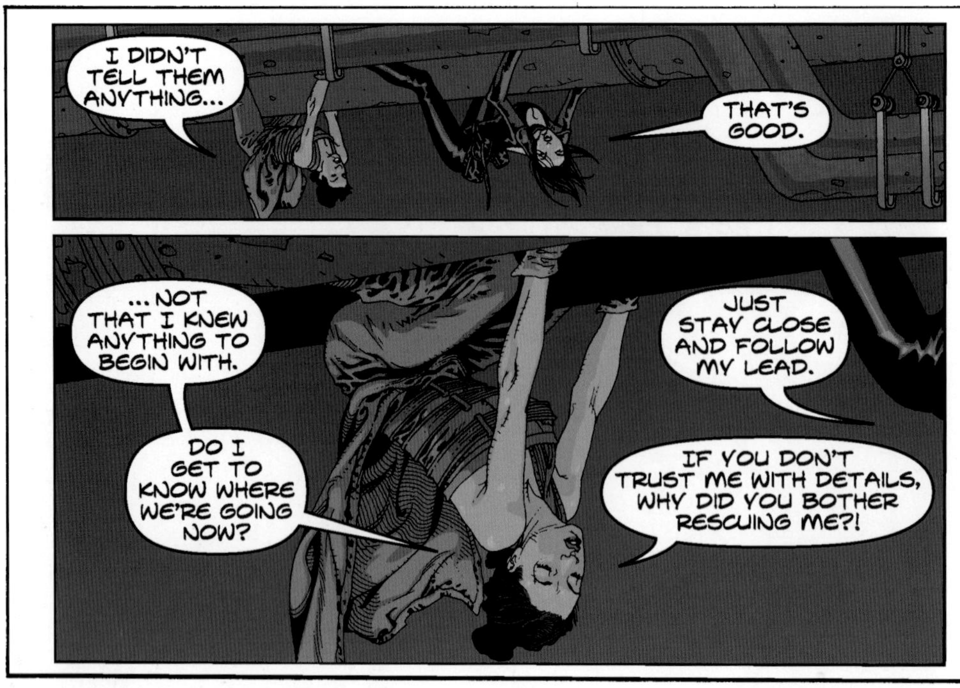
I DIDN'T TELL THEM ANYTHING...
THAT'S GOOD.
...NOT THAT I KNEW ANYTHING TO BEGIN WITH.
JUST STAY CLOSE AND FOLLOW MY LEAD.
DO I GET TO KNOW WHERE WE'RE GOING NOW?
IF YOU DON'T TRUST ME WITH DETAILS, WHY DID YOU BOTHER RESCUING ME?!

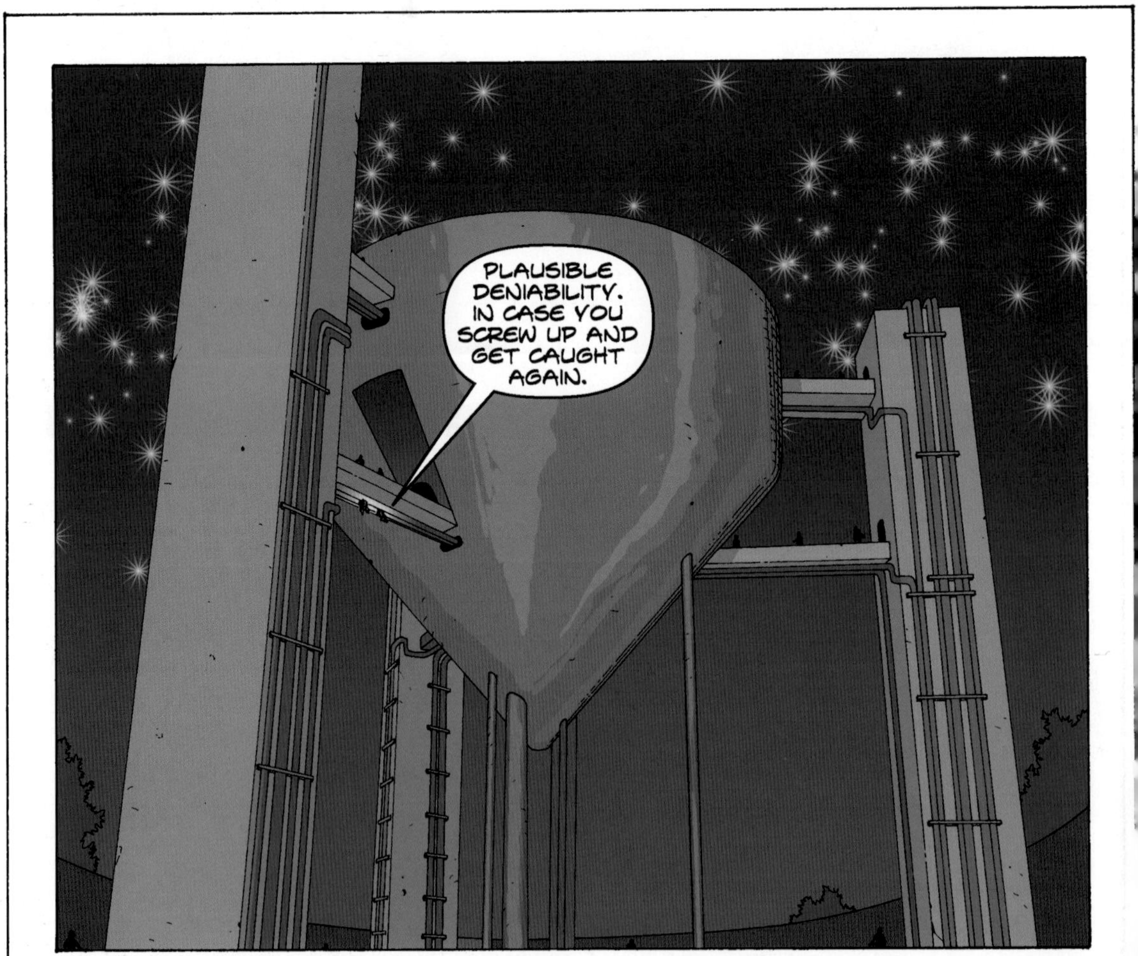
PLAUSIBLE DENIABILITY. IN CASE YOU SCREW UP AND GET CAUGHT AGAIN.

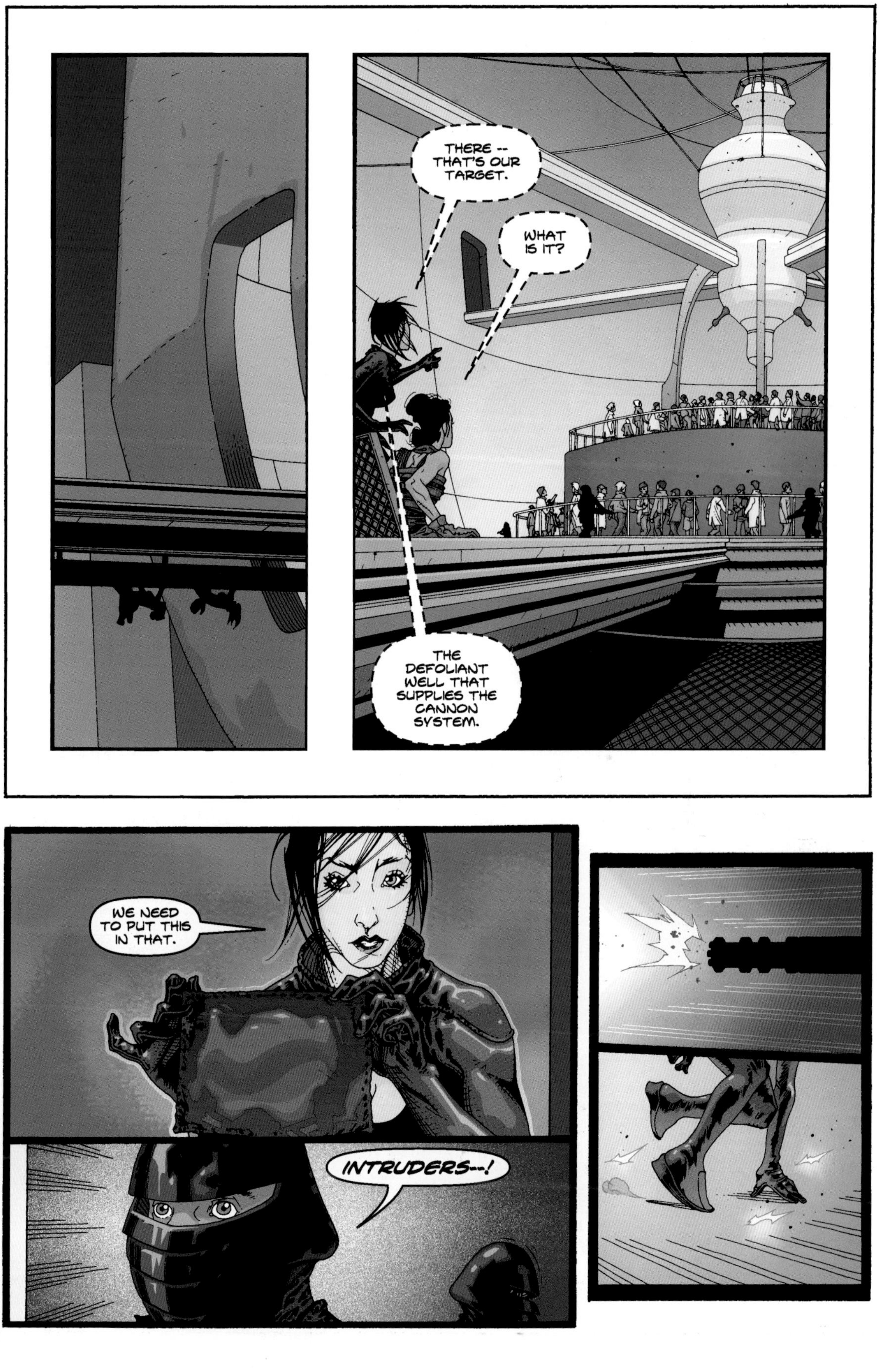

THERE -- THAT'S OUR TARGET.
WHAT IS IT?
THE DEFOLIANT WELL THAT SUPPLIES THE CANNON SYSTEM.
WE NEED TO PUT THIS IN THAT.
INTRUDERS--!

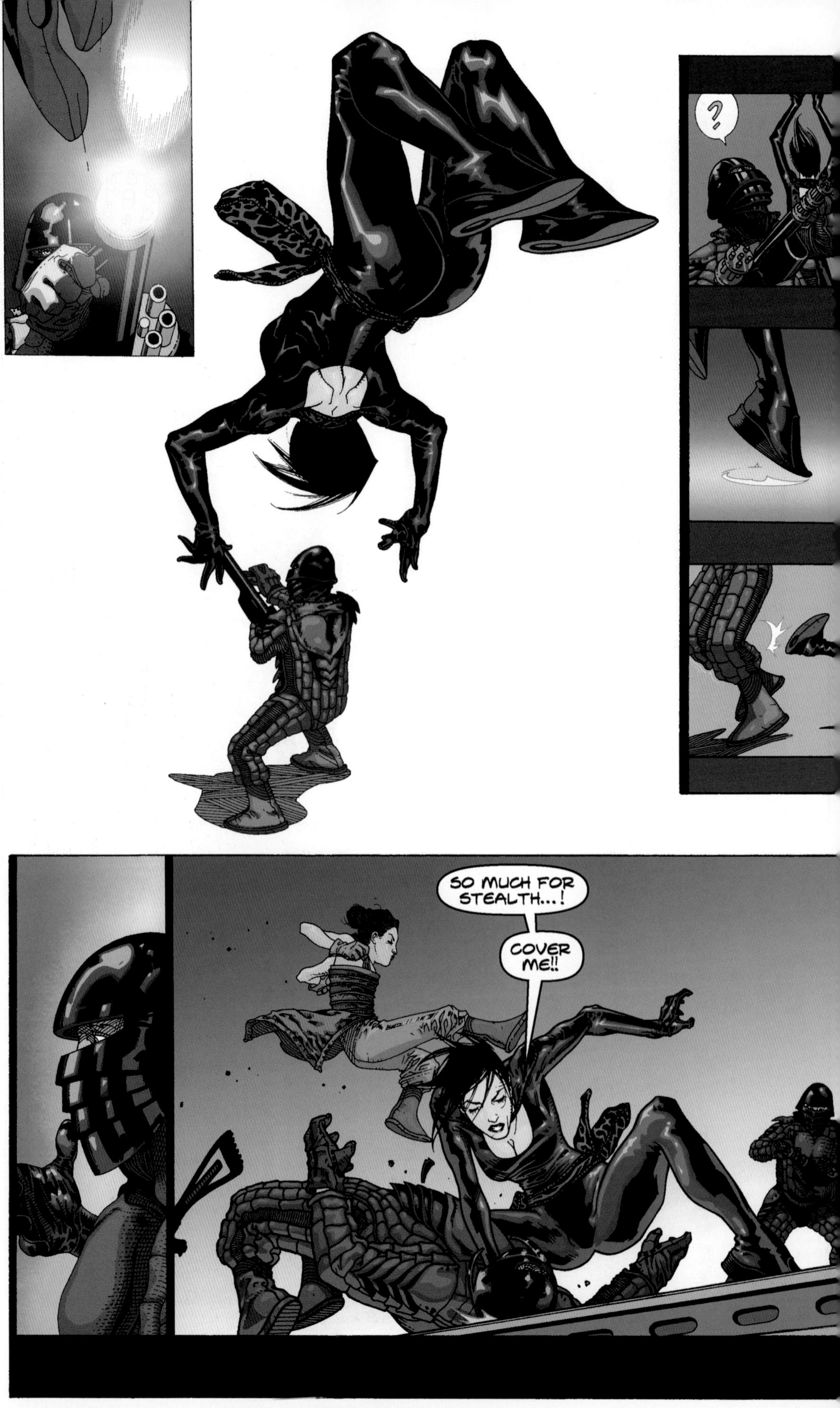

?
SO MUCH FOR STEALTH...!
COVER ME!!

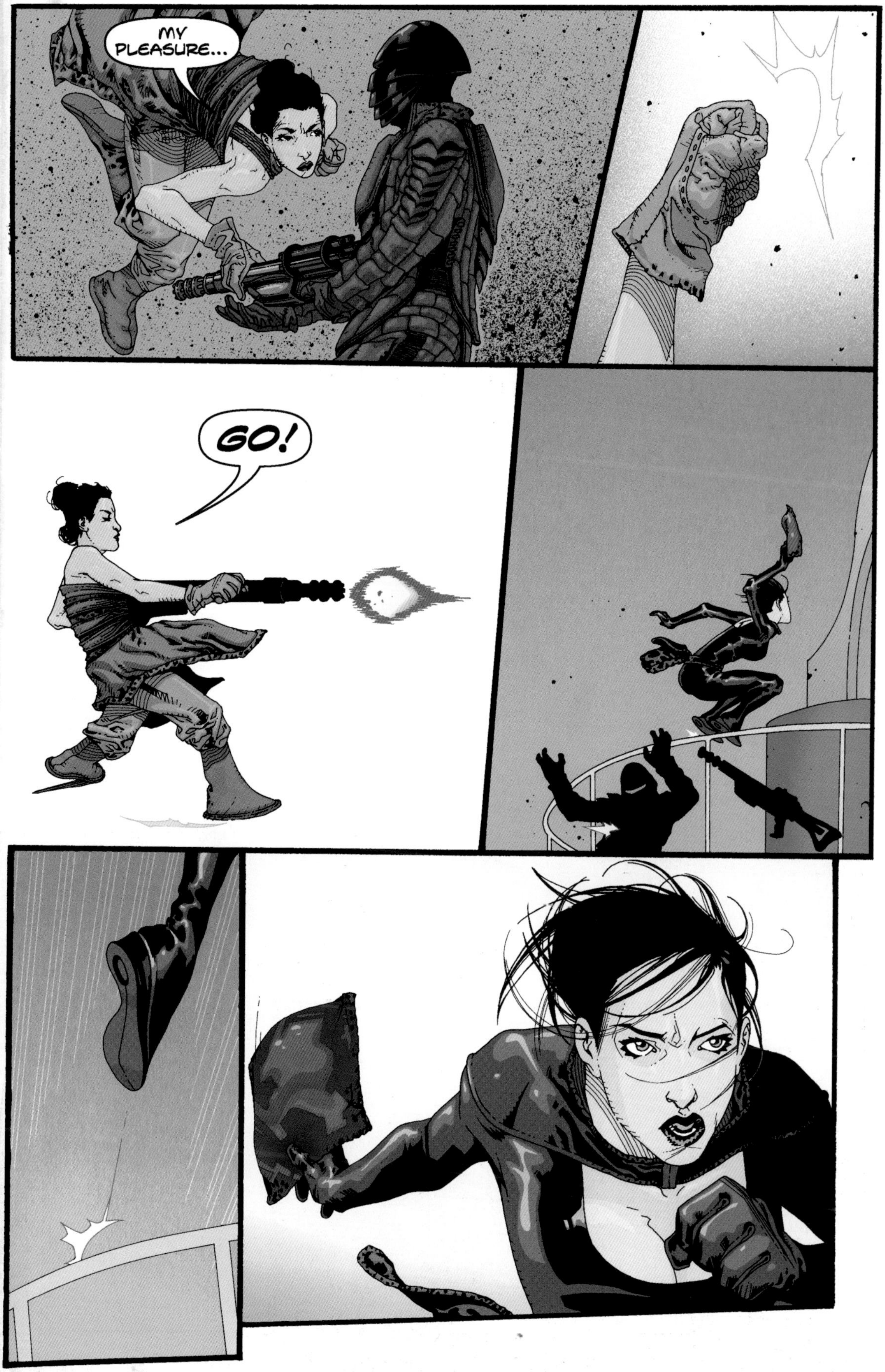
MY PLEASURE...
GO!

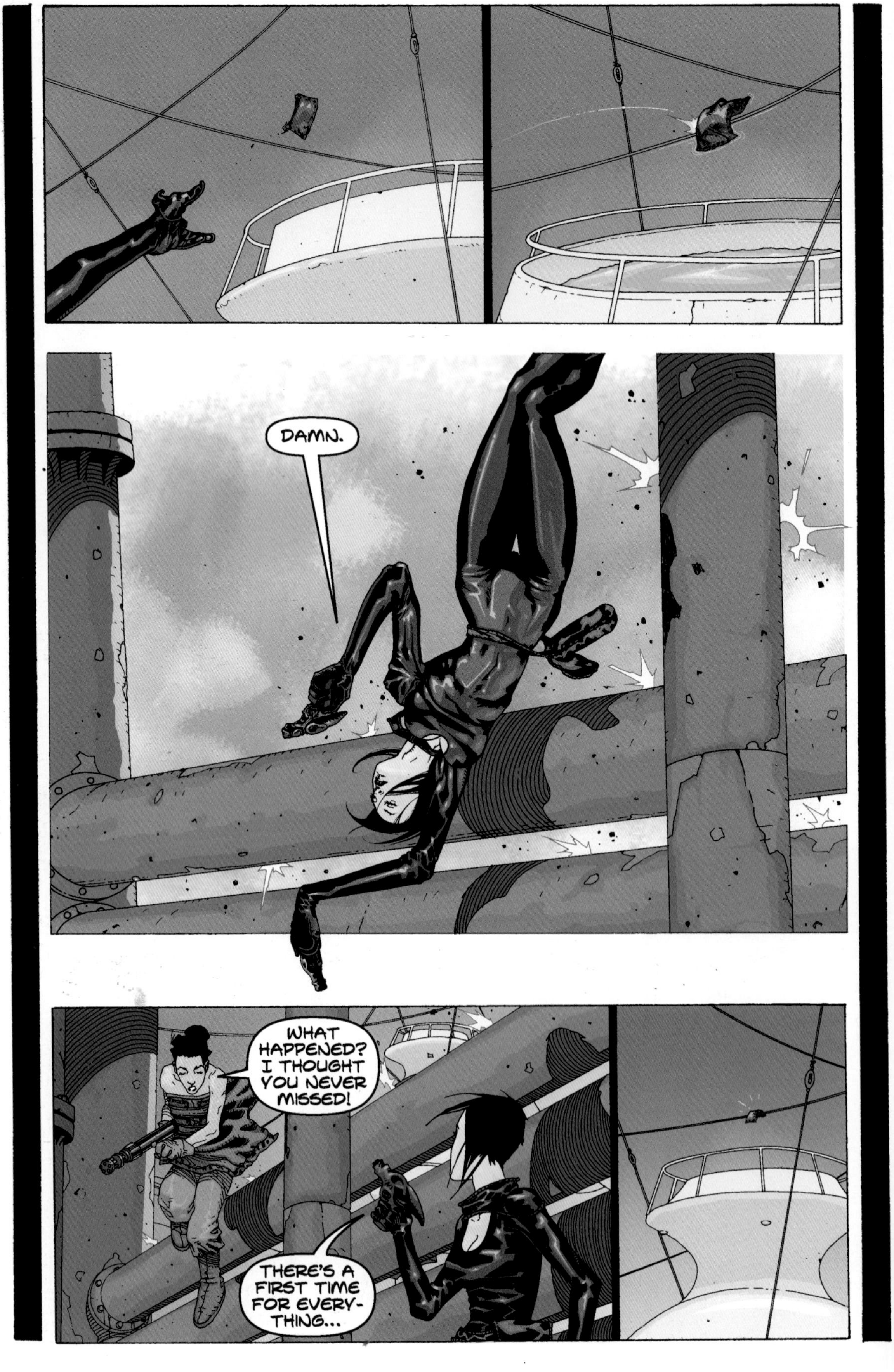
DAMN.
WHAT HAPPENED? I THOUGHT YOU NEVER MISSED!
THERE'S A FIRST TIME FOR EVERY-THING...

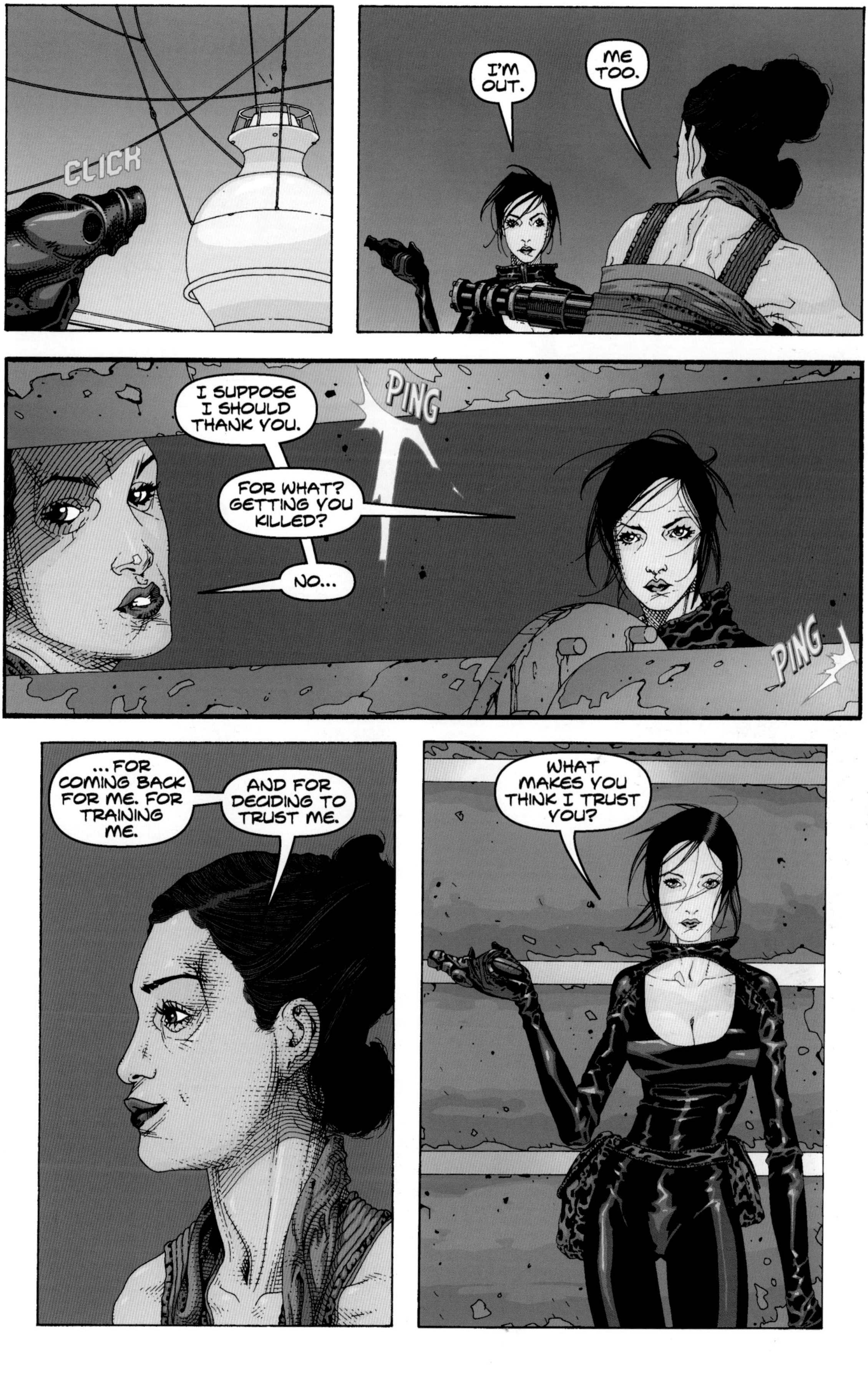
CLICK
I'M OUT.
ME TOO.
I SUPPOSE I SHOULD THANK YOU.
PING
FOR WHAT? GETTING YOU KILLED?
NO...
PING
...FOR COMING BACK FOR ME. FOR TRAINING ME.
AND FOR DECIDING TO TRUST ME.
WHAT MAKES YOU THINK I TRUST YOU?

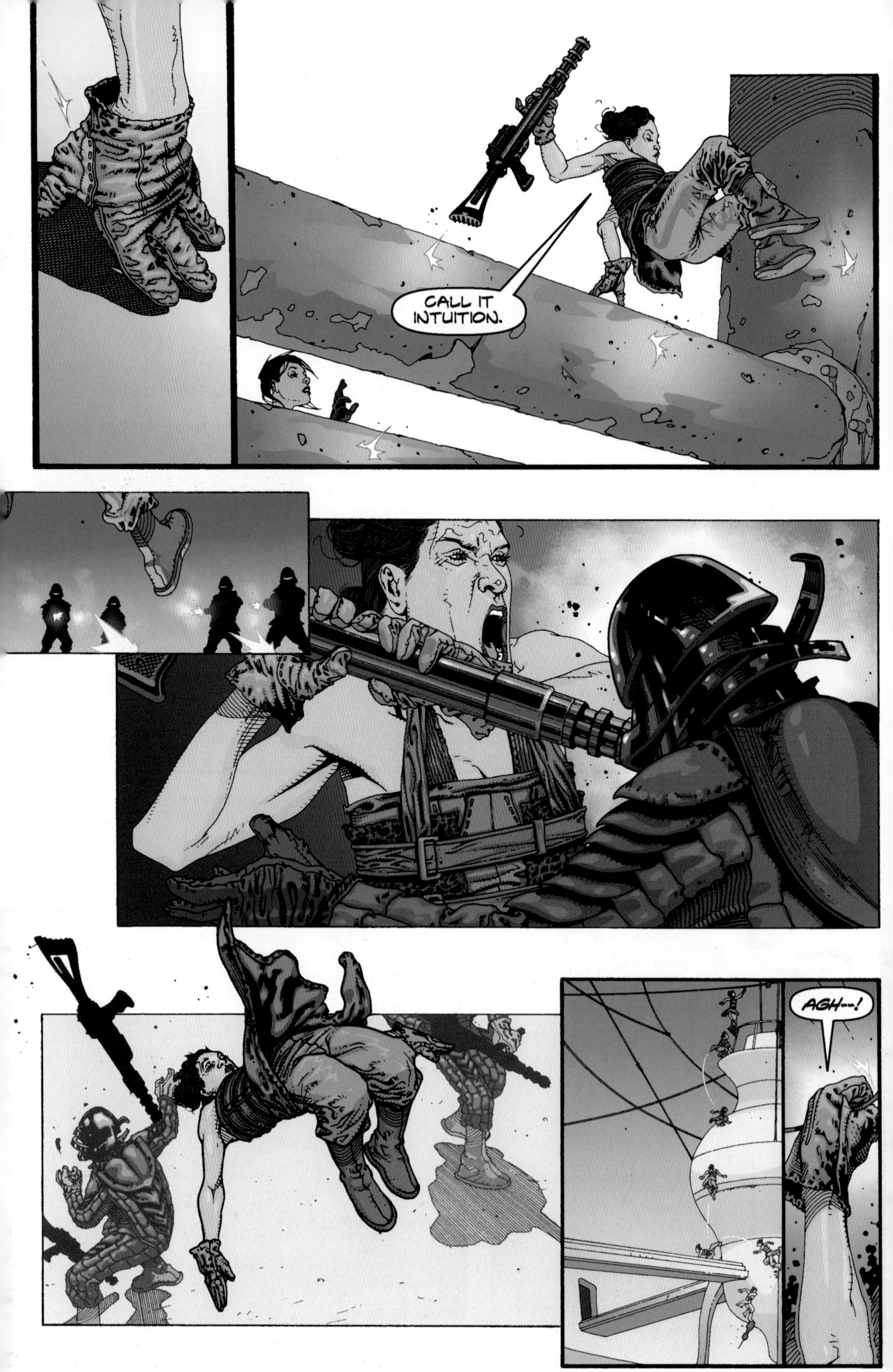
CALL IT INTUITION.
AGH--!

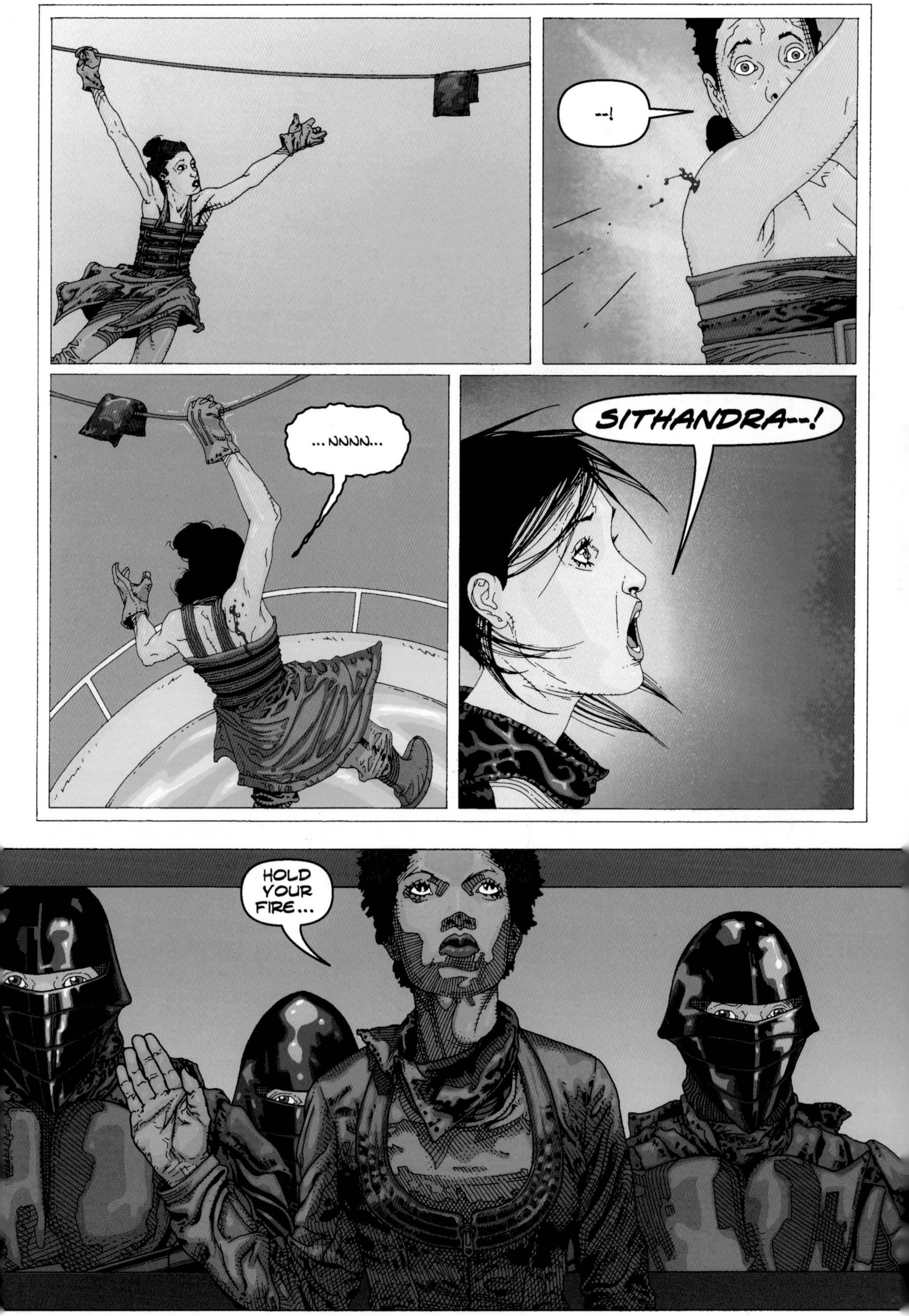
--!
...NNNN...
SITHANDRA--!
HOLD YOUR FIRE...

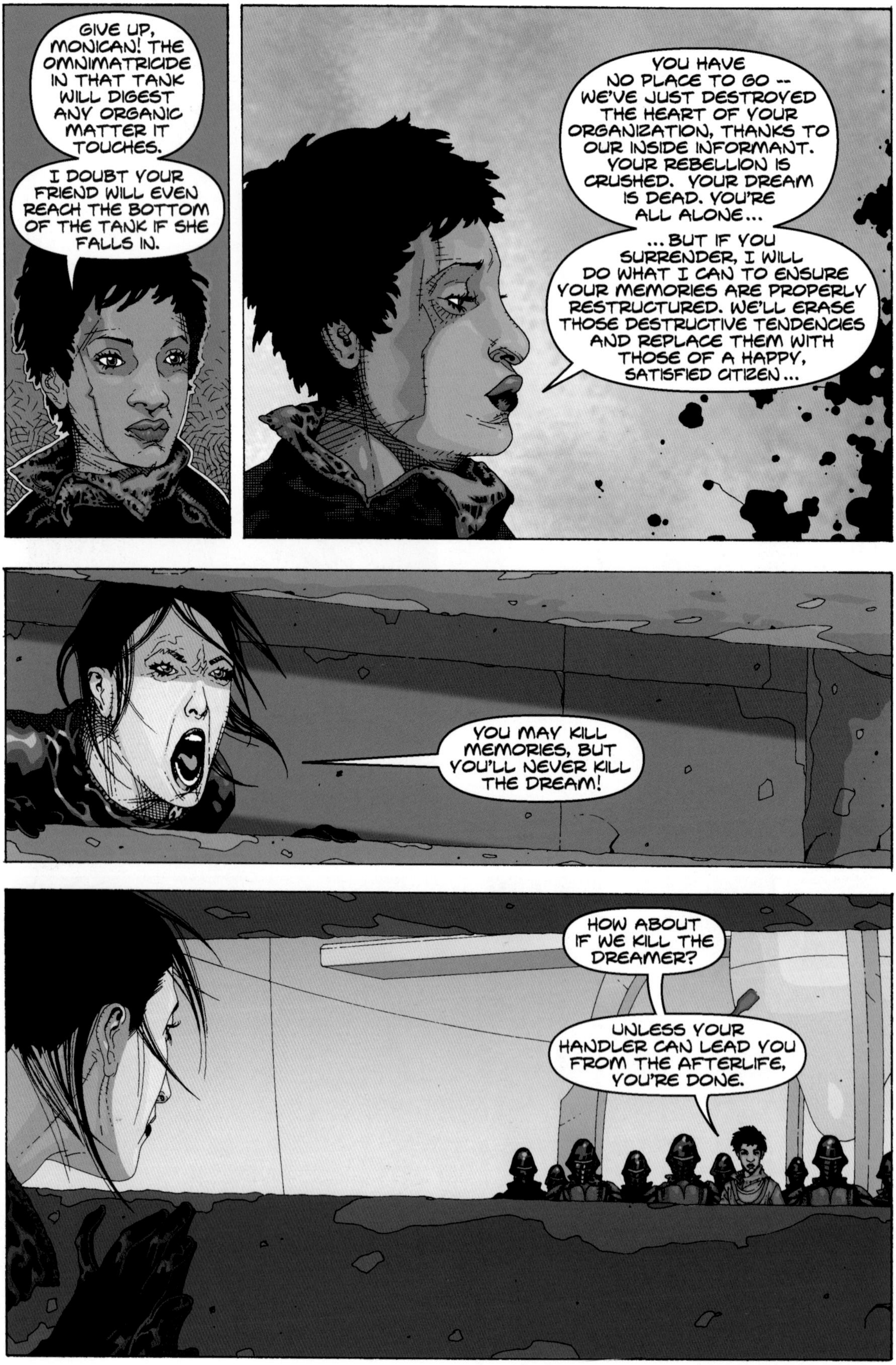
GIVE UP, MONICAN! THE OMNIMATRICIDE IN THAT TANK WILL DIGEST ANY ORGANIC MATTER IT TOUCHES.
I DOUBT YOUR FRIEND WILL EVEN REACH THE BOTTOM OF THE TANK IF SHE FALLS IN.
YOU HAVE NO PLACE TO GO -- WE'VE JUST DESTROYED THE HEART OF YOUR ORGANIZATION, THANKS TO OUR INSIDE INFORMANT. YOUR REBELLION IS CRUSHED. YOUR DREAM IS DEAD. YOU'RE ALL ALONE...
...BUT IF YOU SURRENDER, I WILL DO WHAT I CAN TO ENSURE YOUR MEMORIES ARE PROPERLY RESTRUCTURED. WE'LL ERASE THOSE DESTRUCTIVE TENDENCIES AND REPLACE THEM WITH THOSE OF A HAPPY, SATISFIED CITIZEN...
YOU MAY KILL MEMORIES, BUT YOU'LL NEVER KILL THE DREAM!
HOW ABOUT IF WE KILL THE DREAMER?
UNLESS YOUR HANDLER CAN LEAD YOU FROM THE AFTERLIFE, YOU'RE DONE.

ARE YOU JOKING...?

...SHE PRACTICALLY CREATED THE AFTER-LIFE!

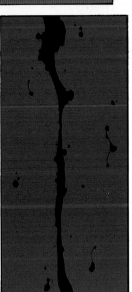

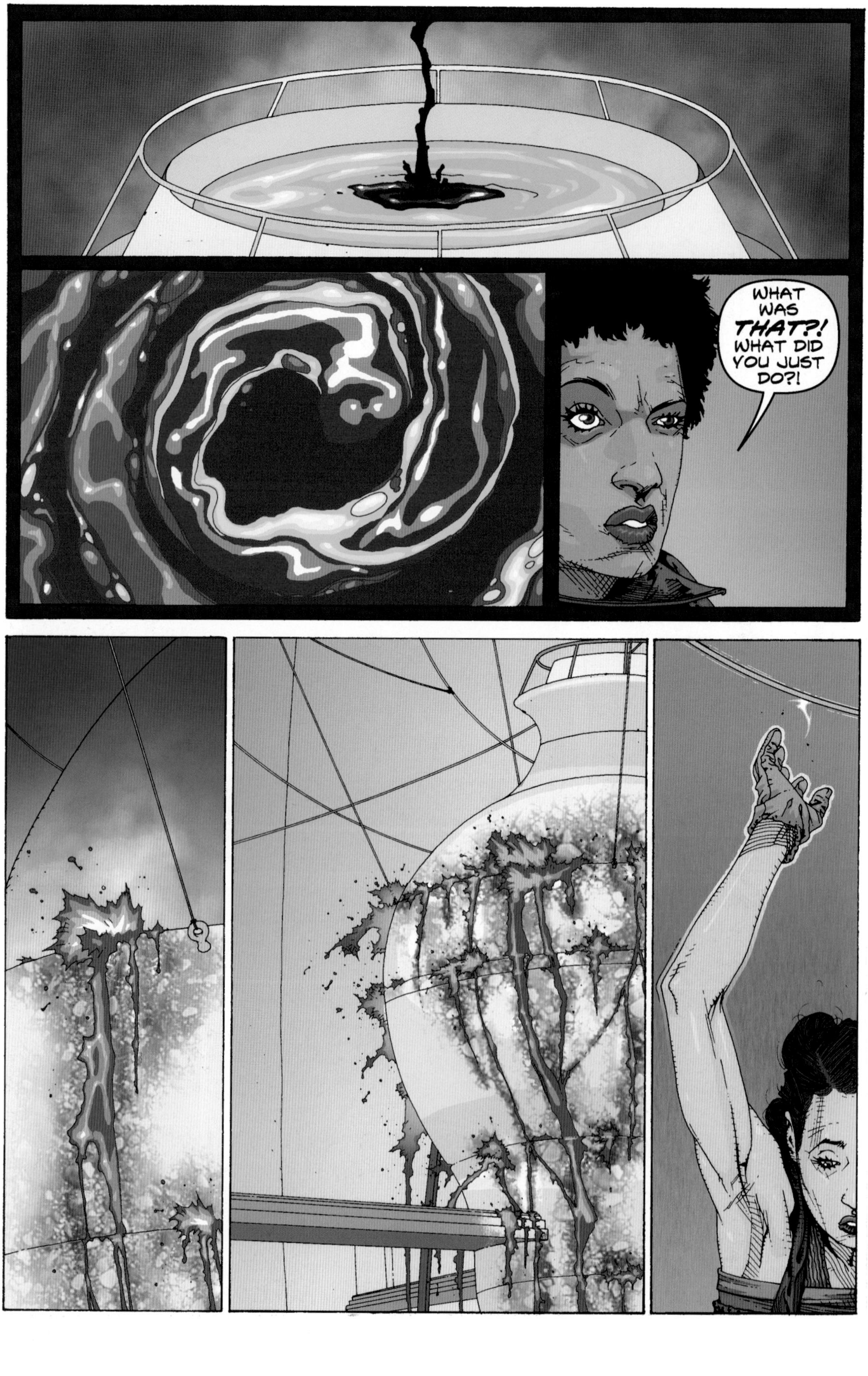
WHAT WAS THAT?! WHAT DID YOU JUST DO?!

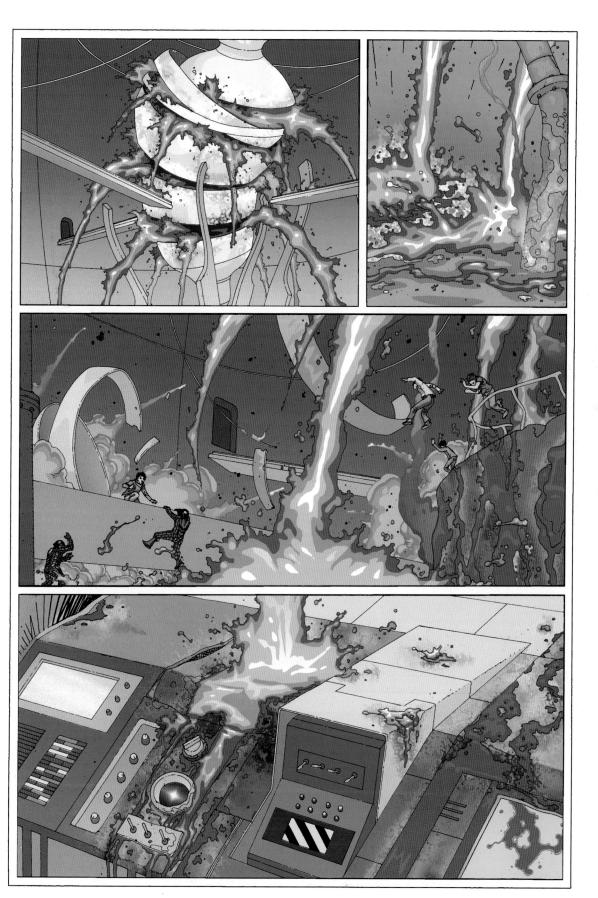

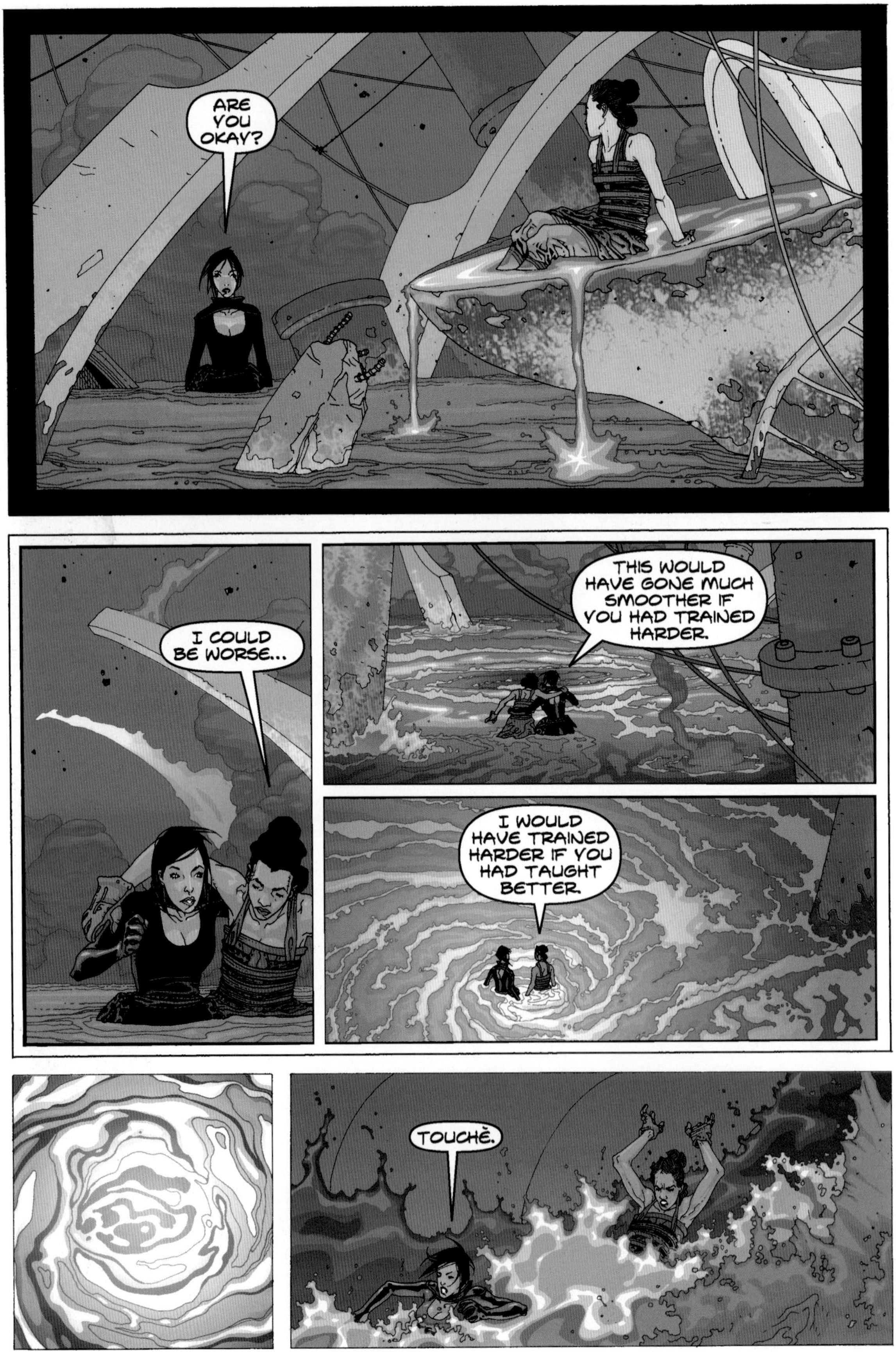

ARE YOU OKAY?
I COULD BE WORSE...
THIS WOULD HAVE GONE MUCH SMOOTHER IF YOU HAD TRAINED HARDER.
I WOULD HAVE TRAINED HARDER IF YOU HAD TAUGHT BETTER.
TOUCHÈ.

ALL IN ALL, A RESPECTABLE SUCCESS.

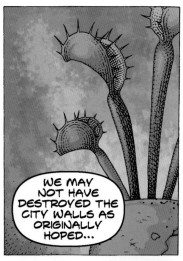

WE MAY NOT HAVE DESTROYED THE CITY WALLS AS ORIGINALLY HOPED...

...BUT WE DID DESTROY THE DEFOLIANT CANNONS, WHICH WILL NOT ONLY PUT A SERIOUS FINANCIAL CRIMP IN THE GOVERNMENT'S MILITARY BUDGET...

...BUT GIVE THE POPULATION A NICE BREAK FROM THE MADDENING, HOURLY DETONATIONS.

ANOTHER JOB WELL DONE.

I ONLY WISH I COULD HAVE KEPT THEM FROM FINDING YOU.

THEY FOUND MY BODY, BUT THEY NEVER FOUND ME.

I KNEW THEY WOULD NOT GIVE UP UNTIL THEY BELIEVED THE REBELLION WAS CRUSHED, SO I LET THEM CRUSH WHAT THEY BELIEVED WAS THE REBELLION.

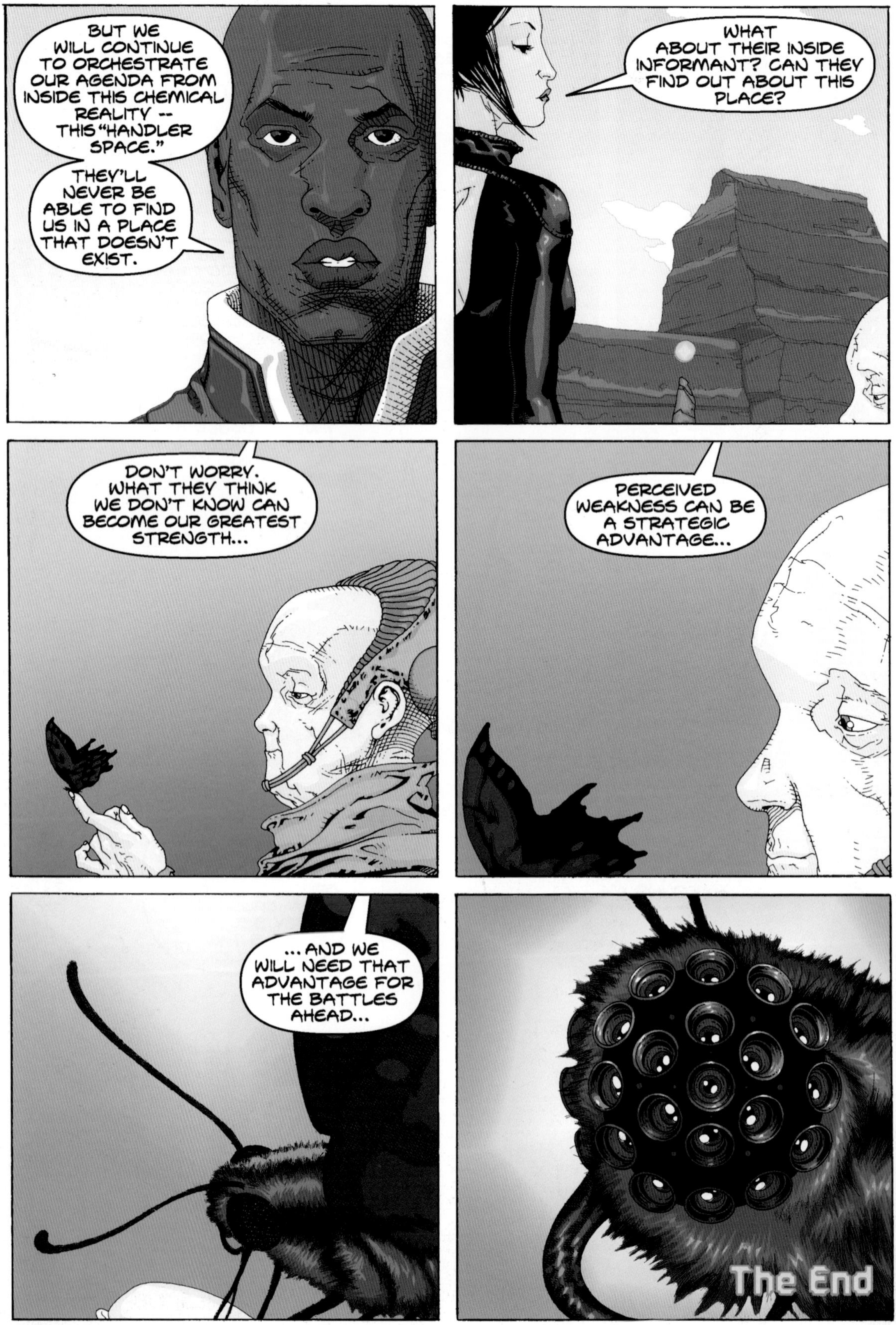
BUT WE WILL CONTINUE TO ORCHESTRATE OUR AGENDA FROM INSIDE THIS CHEMICAL REALITY -- THIS "HANDLER SPACE."
THEY'LL NEVER BE ABLE TO FIND US IN A PLACE THAT DOESN'T EXIST.
WHAT ABOUT THEIR INSIDE INFORMANT? CAN THEY FIND OUT ABOUT THIS PLACE?
DON'T WORRY. WHAT THEY THINK WE DON'T KNOW CAN BECOME OUR GREATEST STRENGTH...
PERCEIVED WEAKNESS CAN BE A STRATEGIC ADVANTAGE...
...AND WE WILL NEED THAT ADVANTAGE FOR THE BATTLES AHEAD...
The End

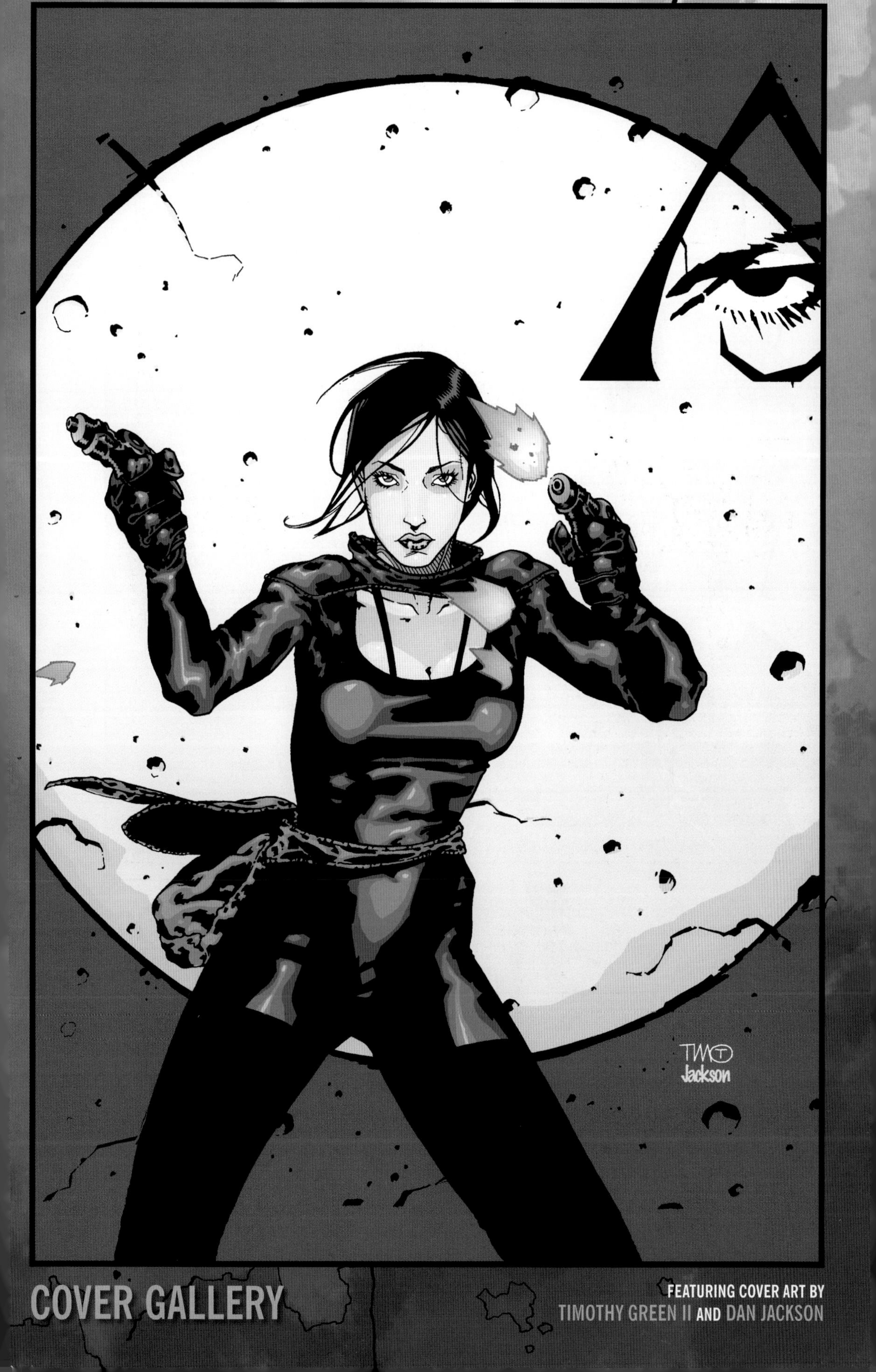
TWO
Jackson

COVER GALLERY

FEATURING COVER ART BY
TIMOTHY GREEN II AND DAN JACKSON

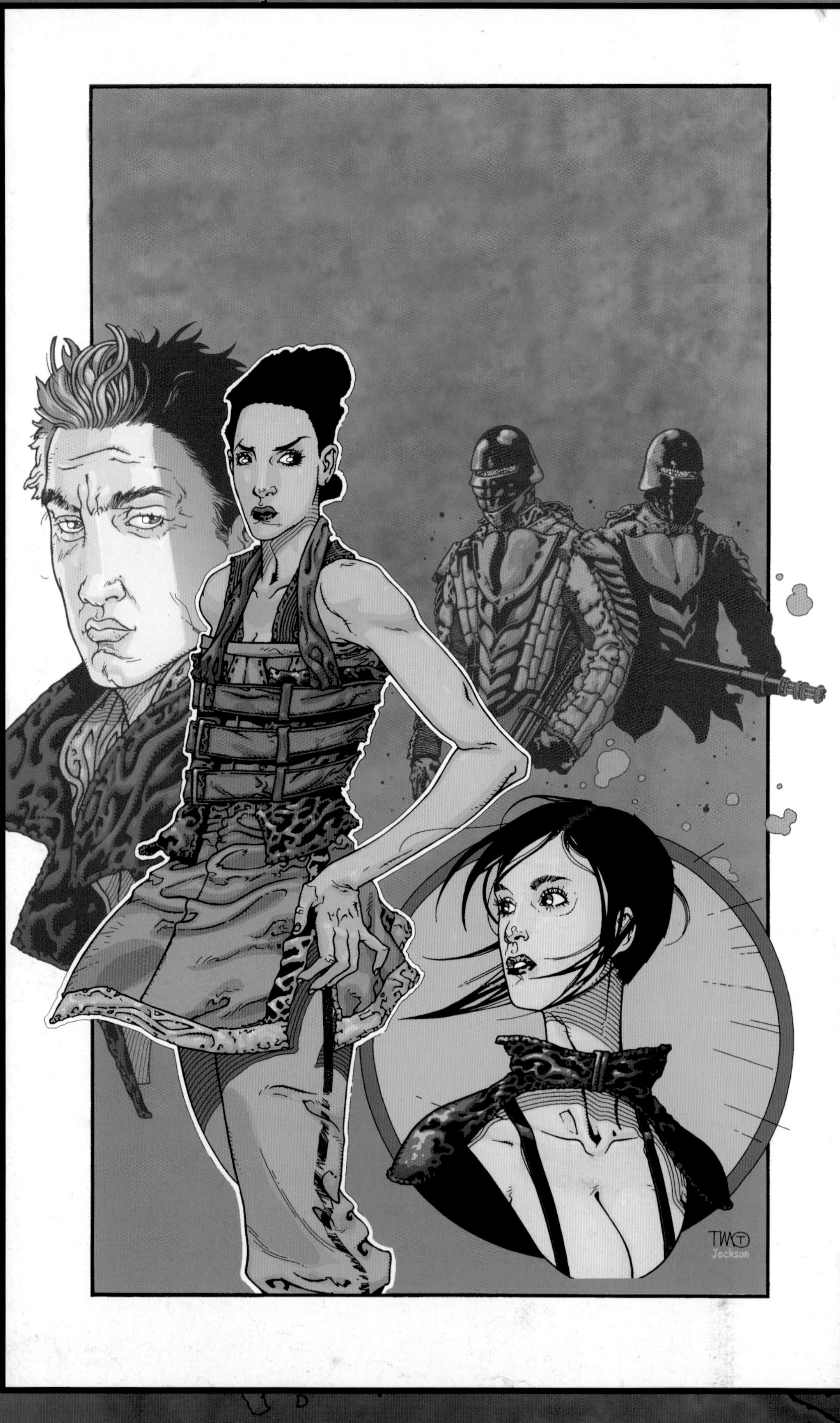
Jackson

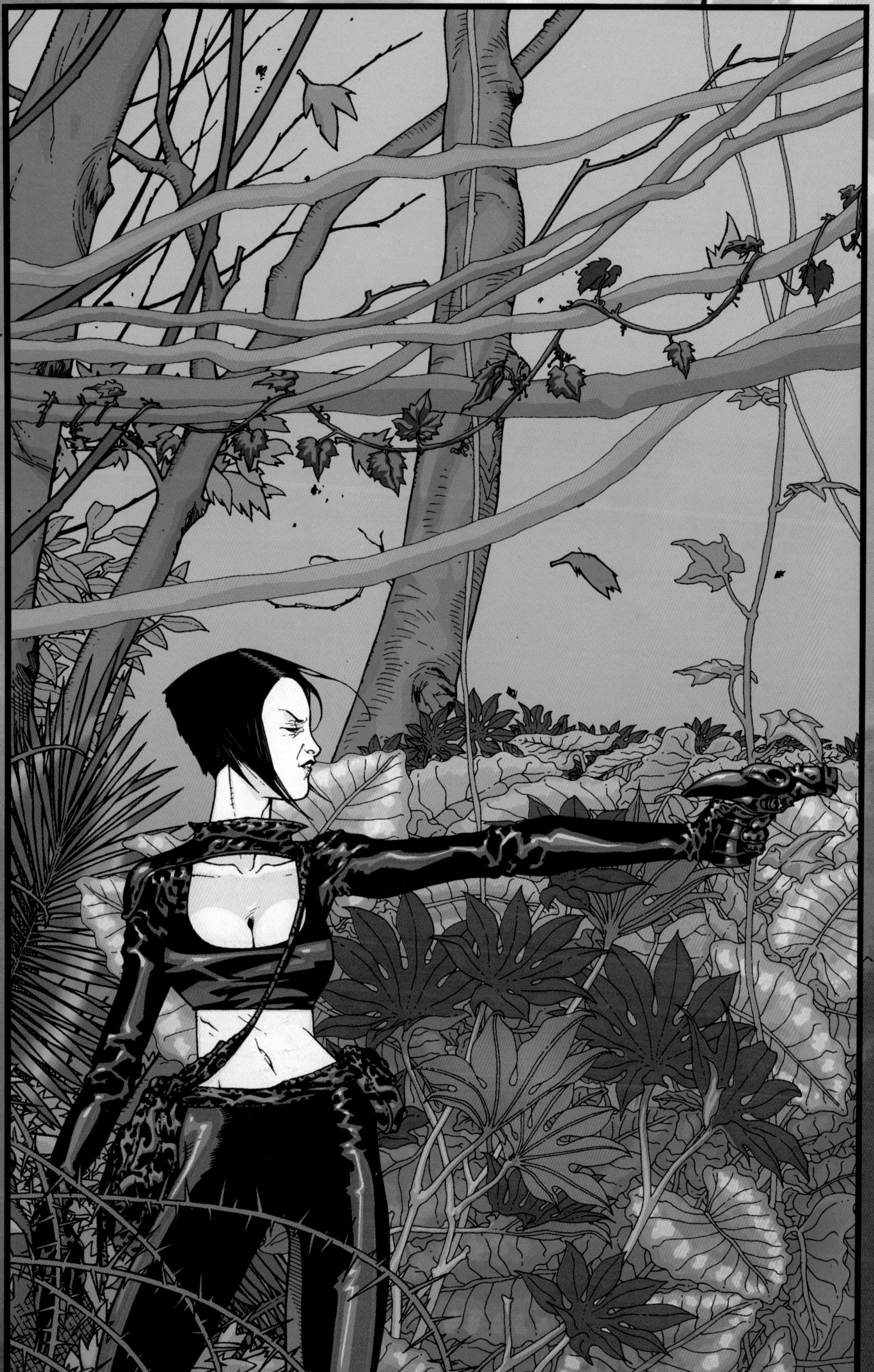

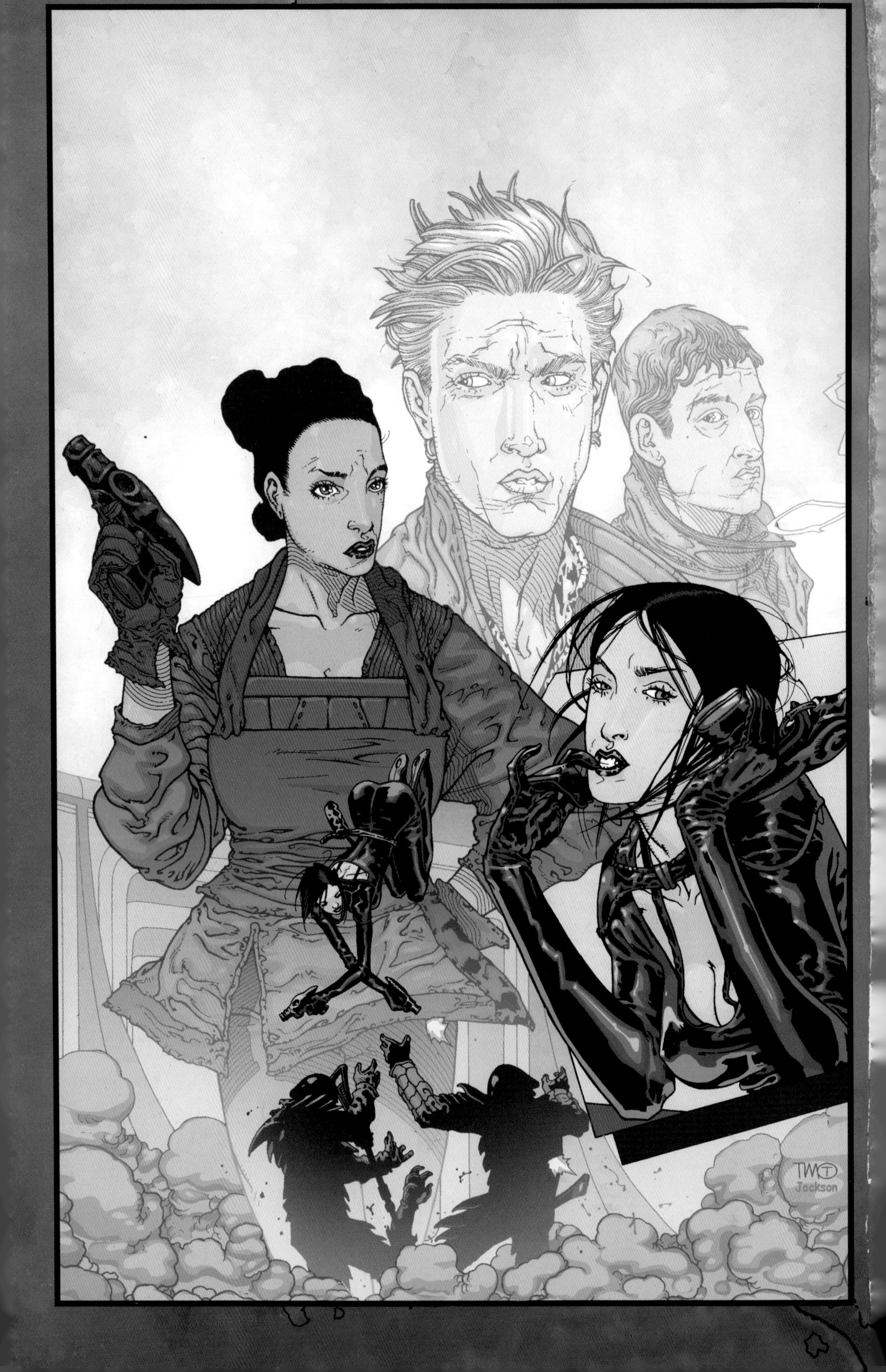
Jackson